"*Building Assets, Reducing Risks* is a key factor in the academic success of high school students. . . . The number one reason that a student doesn't graduate from high school in four years is because they failed a ninth-grade class. Then the student begins tenth grade behind the eight ball, having to take that ninth-grade class plus all of their tenth-grade classes. It's then very difficult to catch up. *Building Assets, Reducing Risks* focuses on the failure rate and getting that as low as possible. That's what it does."

—Rob Metz, *Superintendent, St. Louis Park High School, Minnesota*

"From a parent perspective, we get to see that the teachers are really connecting with the students. . . . They take an interest in students above and beyond academics. . . . The relationship building is huge. To me, that's what makes it—when my kids come home and they are so excited because a teacher gave them a nickname. From then on, math is awesome and they are motivated and they're going to work hard and they're going to figure things out."

—Carrie Jennissen, *mother of two students, St. Louis Park, Minnesota*

"This model is the first comprehensive educational innovation I have found that has developed a structure and process to teach, support, and empower administrators, educators, parents, and students around a common, articulated pathway to student success. This evidence-based program provides specific details for bridging and leveraging the use of real-time student data with proven relationship-building strategies and interventions . . . resulting in increased academic achievement and improved student climate."

—Justin Barbeau, *i3 Grant Coordinator, St. Louis Park High School, Minnesota*

"If students feel as though they have some positive attributes or assets, they can latch on to those and really use those to work to their advantage, and it definitely gives them more confidence, more self-esteem, and I think that's the most important part of teaching. You always have to remember to praise students for what they do well instead of always emphasizing what they're not doing."

—Lianna Messier, *first-year English teacher, Sanford, Maine*

"I can't imagine going back to what we used to do. I think the idea of working together in the block with these other teachers who have all the same students I do . . . I think we've opened our profession to work more with each other and talk about assessments and talk about standards we have in the classroom and expectations. . . . Teaming, our block time, planning out how we're going to intervene with kids has been phenomenal."

—Bill Tracy, *social studies teacher, Bucksport, Maine*

BUILDING ASSETS
Reducing Risks

A SCHOOL IMPROVEMENT MODEL FOR GRADES 6–12

CLASSROOM CURRICULUM

VOLUME 1

UPDATED
AND
EXPANDED

Angela Jerabek, M.S.

Listed in SAMHSA's National Registry of Evidence-based Programs and Practices (NREPP) and
recognized by the Collaborative for Academic, Social, and Emotional Learning (CASEL)

Hazelden
Center City, Minnesota 55012
hazelden.org

ISBN: 978-1-61649-511-4

21 20 19   4 5 6

Cover design: Theresa Gedig

Contents

BUILDING ASSETS, REDUCING RISKS

Duplicating this page is illegal. Do not duplicate without publisher's written permission.

V

Acknowledgments

Just as relationships are integral to the development of healthy and thriving young people, relationships have been critical in the development and implementation of the *Building Assets, Reducing Risks* model. The *Building Assets, Reducing Risks* model is the result of extensive collaboration between educators, researchers, parents, students, and multiple organizations.

I want to acknowledge the exceptional staff at St. Louis Park High School in Minnesota. I had the privilege of continuing to work in St Louis Park High School, the building in which *Building Assets, Reducing Risks* originated, as the model was implemented across the country. Although it was a challenge to balance the demands of the day-to-day implementation of *Building Assets, Reducing Risks* at a high school with leading a national school reform effort, the fact that I was consistently surrounded by educators unequivocally committed to having all students thrive was inspirational. I truly believe that the key to revolutionizing the educational landscape is unleashing the power of our educators. The *Building Assets, Reducing Risks* model draws out teachers' natural belief in a positive future for students by training them to look intentionally for student assets and using them strategically. The daily reminders of the talent of educators coupled with their desire to support students were inspirational.

I need to recognize the work and support of Peter Benson, PhD (1946–2011). Dr. Benson was one of the world's leading authorities on positive youth development, serving for more than twenty-five years as president and CEO of Search Institute. Rather than focus on fixing what was wrong with young people, Dr. Benson proposed focusing on what was right—pinpointing the Developmental Assets that kids need to succeed. Peter was a friend and a mentor. He believed the *Building Assets, Reducing Risks* model was the necessary approach to educational reform, and I am honored to continue to share the message he so beautifully championed.

A heartfelt thank-you to my husband, John, and my children, Haley and Jonah, for the patience, support, and understanding they have demonstrated during the process of developing and implementing this undertaking.

How to Use the CD-ROM

This manual comes with a CD-ROM that contains downloadable and printable resources needed for implementing *Building Assets, Reducing Risks*. The resources are in PDF format and can be accessed using Adobe Reader. If you do not have Adobe Reader, you can download it for free at www.adobe.com.

Whenever you see this icon in the manual, this means the resource is located on the CD-ROM.

The CD-ROM resources cannot be modified, but they can be printed for use without concern of copyright infringement. For a complete list of what is contained on the CD-ROM, see the list in the back of this manual or the Read Me First document on the CD-ROM.

BUILDING ASSETS, REDUCING RISKS

Duplicating this page is illegal. Do not duplicate without publisher's written permission.

ix

Introduction to
Building Assets, Reducing Risks

What Is *Building Assets, Reducing Risks (BARR)*?

Building Assets, Reducing Risks (BARR) is a strength-based educational model originally created to help students manage the transition to high school. This school improvement model can be implemented successfully in grades 6–12. The two fundamental pillars in *BARR* are (1) creating positive, intentional relationships and (2) using real-time student data in collaborative problem-solving settings to guide instructional action.

The model consists of four main resources:

1. The Implementation Guide

2. The Classroom Curriculum, also called "I-Time"

3. Training and ongoing support through needs assessments and technical assistance

4. Block Meetings, Risk Review Meetings, and I-Time Activities: A Video Training Program for School Staff

Although the Classroom Curriculum can be used as a stand-alone resource, to implement *BARR* with fidelity and thereby achieve positive outcomes, the curriculum should be used alongside all of the other model components.

BARR's eight interconnected strategies—all grounded in research about what works in education—provide a comprehensive structure through which a school can accomplish any goal it sets.

What Are the Goals of *BARR*?

The model seeks to help youth succeed in school by increasing the overall health of students and by achieving the following goals:

1. Students are earning all course credits toward graduation (reduced academic failure).

2. Students are earning higher achievement scores.

3. Students are becoming more engaged in learning.

BUILDING ASSETS, REDUCING RISKS

Duplicating this page is illegal. Do not duplicate without publisher's written permission.

1

4. Students are reducing adverse effects of alcohol and other drugs.

5. Teachers are increasing their effectiveness.

Who Is the Intended Audience?

BARR can be used in a variety of school settings: public, private, or charter; large or small; rural, urban, or suburban. Research has been completed on this model for ninth graders as they enter high school, but the model has been successfully implemented in grades 6–12. Where necessary, the I-Time curriculum suggests adaptations of the sessions for younger students.

Is *BARR* an Evidence-Based Model?

The *BARR* model was developed more than eighteen years ago in a St. Louis Park (Minnesota) high school in response to high failure and dropout rates of ninth-grade students. At the time of this publication, it is implemented in eighty schools in thirteen states across the country. With federal funding from the "Investing in Innovation" (i3) program, *BARR* has been rigorously studied using a randomized controlled trial (RCT) in eleven schools of varying locales and geographic regions to better understand the broader context under which *BARR* impacts students transitioning to the ninth grade. This current study is a multisite-within-school RCT that explores replication of *BARR* across three cohorts of schools.

Results from the first RCT demonstrated positive impact on ninth-grade students' standardized test scores, credits earned, and overall failure rate. Carried out in a large urban school in 2011–2012, ninth-grade students who were randomly assigned to participate in *BARR* earned statistically more credits, scored higher on both reading and mathematics standardized tests, and had fewer course failures than those not assigned to *BARR*. Furthermore, qualitative data collected from *BARR* teachers and counselors suggests that staff felt more connected to students, other teachers, and their schools. After only one year of *BARR* implementation, surveyed teachers also reported higher levels of teacher effectiveness.

In the past several years, *BARR* has earned national recognition from the What Works Clearinghouse for the RCT study as having met evidence-based standards, without reservation and having at least one positive statistically significant finding. *BARR* is included in SAMHSA's National Registry of Evidence-based Programs and Practices (NREPP) and the CASEL Guide for Effective Social and Emotional Learning Programs.

Schools that have implemented *BARR* have been recipients of state and national awards for academic achievement. *BARR* is unique in that it is a social-emotional model that produces significant academic results. It supports students in their successful transition to high school and sets them on a positive trajectory toward graduation and beyond.

How Is *BARR* Different from Other School Improvement Programs?

BARR is a multifaceted educational model that is distinct from other school improvement programs because of its six key principles:

1. Emphasizing the strengths of students
2. Focusing on the whole class
3. Addressing all risk factor issues simultaneously
4. Combining system-wide and individual intervention strategies
5. Coordinating all model strategies
6. Increasing teacher effectiveness

Another strength of this model is that teachers intentionally identify students who can achieve more and then encourage and accelerate them. This model transforms all students' school experience. The students affected through the *BARR* intervention are not just the ones considered "at risk" or the gifted students. All students are encouraged to do their best through intentional relationship building and instructional interventions. Relationships are the key drivers for this model's success.

What Is the Theoretical Base of *BARR*?

The *BARR* educational model is one of the first school-based models that integrates the Developmental Assets framework, Risk and Protective Factors focused on prevention strategies, and the Attribution Theory of Student Motivation. The following is a model of how these theories are integrated into *BARR* at the school and student level, with resulting positive outcomes.

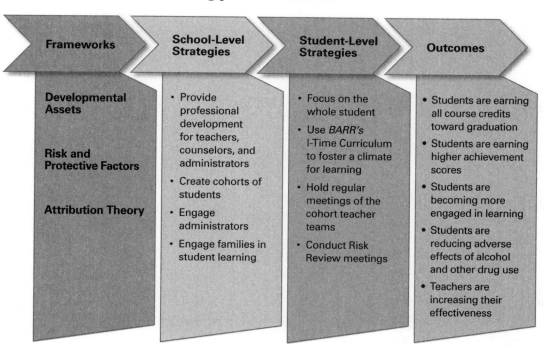

Frameworks	School-Level Strategies	Student-Level Strategies	Outcomes
Developmental Assets Risk and Protective Factors Attribution Theory	• Provide professional development for teachers, counselors, and administrators • Create cohorts of students • Engage administrators • Engage families in student learning	• Focus on the whole student • Use *BARR's* I-Time Curriculum to foster a climate for learning • Hold regular meetings of the cohort teacher teams • Conduct Risk Review meetings	• Students are earning all course credits toward graduation • Students are earning higher achievement scores • Students are becoming more engaged in learning • Students are reducing adverse effects of alcohol and other drug use • Teachers are increasing their effectiveness

What Are Some Things I Should Be Aware of When Using *BARR*?

Here are some helpful tips for using *BARR:*

- Look intentionally for student strengths, integrating these into classroom plans and using them strategically for underachieving students.
- Seek to create a collaborative, problem-solving culture within your block teacher team.
- Talk with your students. Enjoy their company. Get to know them on a personal level.

Introduction to the
Classroom "I-Time" Curriculum, Volume 1

The Classroom Curriculum, also called "I-Time," is a key tool for building assets in students. The term "I-Time" is used because these sessions focus on students learning more about themselves and building personal strengths or assets that will help them become successful in life.

The curriculum includes team-building activities, education in communication and social competencies, and energizers. Students and teachers participate together in specific activities around a variety of topics.

I-Time activities are designed to be used on a consistent basis throughout the school year for an average of thirty minutes a week. Some activities will require more than thirty minutes, and others will require less. The approximate time needed is noted in each

> The purpose of I-Time is to create a positive school climate by engaging students and teachers in activities to build individual and group strength.

session. The critical aspect is to have I-Time offered consistently once every week regardless of the length of any given activity. These weekly I-Time sessions are taught by one of the *BARR* block teachers, typically rotating, so each teacher does an I-Time session approximately every three weeks.

There are ten main sections or topic areas in volume 1 with a total of thirty-seven I-Time sessions. Starting on page 179, there are directions for energizer activities designed to fill a thirty-minute class period if an I-Time activity is completed early or to serve as short I-Time activities if needed. The energizers are important, fun activities that encourage physical movement and engage the students. Many students are more willing to participate in heavier content areas after participating in the fun energizer activities.

I-Time Tips for Success

- The sessions can be adapted to meet classroom needs. However, if sessions are adapted, make sure the key content is still covered.

- I-Time sections are sequential. It is recommended that I-Time sections be completed in the order presented, unless a session within a section complements a content area from another class (for example, the I-Time section on diversity could be offered while simultaneously discussing diversity in a social studies class).

- During I-Time sessions, encourage students to discuss their thoughts or feelings in small groups. Students are usually more willing to share in a small-group setting, which encourages much broader participation from all class members. Then have small discussion groups report back to the larger class to stimulate a richer class discussion.

- When using the I-Time sessions, identify class members as "participants" and "facilitator" rather than as "students" and "teacher." Although teachers will be facilitating the sessions, they are encouraged to actively engage in all activities as "participants" as well. A critical aspect of I-Time is for students to build a relationship with their block or team teachers. This requires willingness on the part of the teachers to share of themselves in order to foster relationship building.

- If the entire grade is structured in a block or team system, try to work through some sessions and energizer activities (such as field days) when all the blocks (teachers and classes) are together.

- Note that each I-Time session refers to the asset categories and to risk and protective factors being addressed in the session. (See appendix 1 and appendix 2 of the Implementation Guide for more information.)

- I-Time sessions are constructed for students in grades 9–12, but where applicable, adaptations for grades 6–8 are listed at the end of each session. Feel free to make further adaptations according to your class's ability level.

This is not a traditional curriculum. Although there is information you want to share with students, these sessions are designed to establish communication and build relationships among all members of your class. As such, remember that you are more of a facilitator than teacher, and you will take part in the activities alongside the students. Try to focus more on the interaction among students and yourself, rather than on conveying a body of content.

Quick Tips

- Be an attentive listener.
- Make sure all viewpoints are heard.
- Make sure everyone has the opportunity to speak.
- Guide discussions so no one participant dominates the conversation.
- Establish an environment where all participant voices are respected and confidentiality is respected.
- Consistently identify participants' assets and strengths.

"At a time when the traditional structures of caring have deteriorated, schools must become places where facilitators and students live together, talk with each other, take delight in each other's company. My guess is that when schools focus on what really matters in life, the cognitive ends we now pursue so painfully and artificially will be achieved somewhat more naturally.

. . . It is obvious that children will work harder and do things—even odd things like adding fractions—for people they love and trust."

Nel Noddings, "Schools Face 'Crisis in Caring,'" *Education Week,* December 7, 1988, www.edweek.org/ew/articles/1988/12/07/08100011.h08.html. Reprinted with permission from the author.

7

I-Time Scope and Sequence

Section	The purpose of each section is . . .
SECTION 1: Building a Connected Community	• to establish rules for creating a respectful community within the classroom • to build community in the classroom by learning participants' names and anecdotal information about others • to help participants develop an understanding of other participants and their commonalities • to help participants become more acquainted with one another, having peers introduce participants to the entire class • to provide an opportunity for participants and staff to develop relationships beyond just a surface level • to build conversation skills • to learn that an effective team requires individuals to assume various roles
SECTION 2: Goals	• to learn a process for establishing and reaching a goal • to demonstrate the need for goals and dreams • to set personal goals • to understand and practice a decision-making process
SECTION 3: Leadership	• to identify your leadership style • to discover how participants work with people of similar and different leadership styles
SECTION 4: Communication	• to demonstrate the power of nonverbal communication • to recognize the impact of verbal and nonverbal communication on peers • to recognize and understand how feelings affect communication • to identify specific communication methods that are used to achieve a task • to practice methods that will promote effective communication • to teach participants that it's important to identify people in their lives they can trust and to communicate with those people when making important decisions or facing difficult circumstances • to recognize qualities of a good listener • to recognize how individuals can hear the same information yet process it differently and arrive at different conclusions • to develop responding skills • to learn how to say no in tough situations using refusal skills • to identify stress and stress relievers in participants' lives

I-Time Scope and Sequence *continued*

Section	The purpose of each section is . . .
SECTION 5: **Assets Activities**	• to analyze students' own assets and compare their responses to those of national norms • to increase understanding of the Developmental Assets framework • to build skills • to identify sources of support in their lives
SECTION 6: **Grief and Loss**	• to understand the process of grief and loss, exploring its impact on our lives
SECTION 7: **Bullying**	• to raise awareness of bullying and increase sensitivity to others
SECTION 8: **Diversity**	• to understand personal values and values of others • to understand how gender roles affect our lives • to identify strengths and areas of needed improvements in your school
SECTION 9: **Risky Behavior**	• to recognize high-risk behavior • to recognize health-compromising risky behavior • to create positive alternatives to risky behaviors • to recognize a substance use disorder and acquire knowledge about alcohol and other drugs • to understand enabling • to identify and recognize the importance of circles of support
SECTION 10: **Dreams**	• to strengthen a positive self-identity • to bring a sense of closure to the year • to celebrate the end of the semester, reminding participants of I-Time activities that occurred during the year

Related National Academic Standards

Using *Building Assets, Reducing Risks* will help you meet the following national academic standards:

Health Standards

Knows environmental and external factors that affect individual and community health

Level III (Grade 6–8)

- Knows cultural beliefs, socioeconomic considerations, and other environmental factors within a community that influence the health of its members
- Understands how various messages from the media, peers, and other sources impact health practices
- Understands how peer relationships affect health

Level IV (Grade 9–12)

- Knows how the health of individuals can be influenced by the community
- Understands how the prevention and control of health problems are influenced by research and medical advances
- Understands how cultural diversity enriches and challenges health behaviors

Knows how to maintain mental and emotional health

Level III (Grade 6–8)

- Knows strategies to manage stress and feelings caused by disappointment, separation, or loss
- Knows characteristics and conditions associated with positive self-esteem
- Knows appropriate ways to build and maintain positive relationships with peers, parents, and other adults (e.g., interpersonal communication)
- Understands the difference between safe and risky or harmful behaviors in relationships
- Knows techniques for seeking help and support through appropriate resources

BUILDING ASSETS, REDUCING RISKS

Duplicating this page is illegal. Do not duplicate without publisher's written permission.

11

Level IV (Grade 9–12)

- Knows skills used to communicate effectively with family, friends, and others, and the effects of open and honest communication
- Knows strategies for coping with and overcoming feelings of rejection, social isolation, and other forms of stress
- Understands the role of denial as a negative influence on mental and emotional health, and ways to overcome denial and seek assistance when needed

Understands aspects of substance use and abuse

Level III (Grade 6–8)

- Knows conditions that may put people at higher risk for substance abuse problems
- Knows factors involved in the development of a drug dependency and the early, observable signs and symptoms
- Knows the short- and long-term consequences of the use of alcohol, tobacco, and other drugs
- Knows community resources that are available to assist people with alcohol, tobacco, and other drug problems

Level IV (Grade 9–12)

- Knows the short- and long-term effects associated with the use of alcohol, tobacco, and other drugs on reproduction, pregnancy, and the health of children
- Knows how the abuse of alcohol, tobacco, and other drugs often plays a role in dangerous behavior and can have adverse consequences on the community
- Understands that alcohol, tobacco, and other drug dependencies are treatable diseases/conditions

Understands the fundamental concepts of growth and development

Level III (Grade 6–8)

- Knows strategies for coping with concerns and stress related to the changes that occur during adolescence

Life Skills Standards

Thinking and Reasoning
Applies decision-making techniques

Level III (Grade 6–8)

- Identifies situations in the community and in one's personal life in which a decision is required
- Secures factual information needed to evaluate alternatives and uses it to predict the consequences of selecting each alternative
- Identifies the values underlying the alternatives that are considered and the criteria that will be used to make a selection among the alternatives
- Analyzes personal decisions in terms of the options that were considered
- Uses a decision-making grid or matrix to make or study decisions involving a relatively limited number of alternatives and criteria

Level IV (Grade 9–12)

- Uses a decision-making grid or matrix to make or study decisions involving a relatively large number of alternatives and criteria
- Evaluates major factors (e.g., personal priorities, environmental conditions, peer groups) that influence personal decisions
- Analyzes the impact of decisions on self and others and takes responsibility for consequences and outcomes of decisions

Working with Others
Contributes to the overall effort of a group

Level IV (Grade K–12)

- Knows the behaviors and skills that contribute to team effectiveness
- Works cooperatively within a group to complete tasks, achieve goals, and solve problems
- Demonstrates respect for others' rights, feelings, and points of view in a group
- Identifies and uses the individual strengths and interests of others to accomplish team goals
- Helps the group establish goals, taking personal responsibility for accomplishing such goals
- Evaluates the overall progress of a group toward a goal
- Contributes to the development of a supportive climate in groups

- Actively listens to the ideas of others and asks clarifying questions
- Takes the initiative in interacting with others
- Uses appropriate strategies when making requests of other people

Uses conflict-resolution techniques

Level IV (Grade K–12)

- Communicates ideas in a manner that does not irritate others
- Understands the impact of criticism on psychological state, emotional state, habitual behavior, and beliefs
- Determines the causes and potential sources of conflicts
- Identifies individual vs. group or organizational interests in conflicts (e.g., works to build consensus within a group while maintaining minority viewpoints)

Works well with diverse individuals and in diverse situations

Level IV (Grade K–12)

- Works well with those of the opposite gender, of differing abilities, and from different age groups
- Works well with those from different ethnic groups, of different religious orientations, and of cultures different from their own

Displays effective interpersonal communication skills

Level IV (Grade K–12)

- Demonstrates appropriate behaviors for relating well with others (e.g., empathy, caring, respect, helping, friendliness, politeness)
- Exhibits positive character traits toward others, including honesty, fairness, dependability, and integrity
- Provides feedback in a constructive manner, and recognizes the importance of seeking and receiving constructive feedback in a non-defensive manner
- Uses nonverbal communication such as eye contact, body position, and gestures effectively
- Demonstrates attentive listening by clarifying messages received (e.g., paraphrasing, questioning)
- Attends to both verbal and nonverbal messages

- Demonstrates sensitivity to cultural diversity (e.g., personal space, use of eye contact, gestures, bias-free language)
- Acknowledges the strengths and achievements of others

Demonstrates leadership skills

Level IV (Grade K–12)

- Understands one's own role as a leader or follower in various situations
- Knows the qualities of good leaders and followers
- Demonstrates and applies leadership skills and qualities (e.g., plans wins and celebrates accomplishments; recognizes the contributions of others; passes on authority when appropriate)

Self-regulation

Sets and manages goals

Level IV (Grade K–12)

- Sets explicit long-term goals and shorter-range sub-goals
- Sets routine goals for improving daily life
- Understands personal wants and needs, and how goal-setting can help one achieve wants and needs
- Displays a sense of personal direction and purpose

Performs self-appraisal

Level IV (Grade K–12)

- Identifies basic values, and distinguishes values from personal preferences, needs, and wants
- Determines appropriate behaviors that are used and should be adopted to obtain wants and/or needs
- Knows personal strengths and weaknesses and techniques for overcoming weaknesses
- Identifies personal motivational patterns, personality characteristics, and style

Considers risks

Level IV (Grade K–12)

- Weighs risks in making decisions and solving problems
- Thinks clearly under stress

BUILDING ASSETS, REDUCING RISKS

Duplicating this page is illegal. Do not duplicate without publisher's written permission.

15

Maintains a healthy self-concept

Level IV (Grade K–12)

- Has confidence in one's own abilities, including the ability to succeed
- Uses techniques (e.g., recalling positive things others have said about oneself) to remind self of strengths
- Uses positive affirmations and self-talk to improve sense of self, build confidence, and complete difficult tasks
- Analyzes self-statements for their positive and negative effects
- Uses high self-esteem body language

Source: Mid-continent Research for Education and Learning. *National Health Education Standards.* http://www2.mcrel.org/compendium/browse.asp.

Section 1: Building a Connected Community

Session Title	Session Description	Materials Needed	Preparation Needed
Session 1: House Rules	Through discussion, brainstorming, and voting, participants will establish rules for creating a respectful community within the classroom.	• Whiteboard or Smart Board • Markers • Poster board, three to five pieces	• None needed.
Session 2: "Do You Know Your Neighbor?"	Through playing a game and discussion, participants will build a community in their classroom by learning participants' names and anecdotal information about each other.	• Chairs	• Place chairs in a circle, one chair per participant minus one.
Session 3: Commonalities	Through discussion, participants will learn about other participants and their commonalities.	• Commonalities handout • Pens or pencils, one per participant	• Print and copy Commonalities handout, one per participant.
Session 4: Shields	Through activities and discussion, participants become better acquainted with one another and introduce each other to the entire class.	• Shield Interview Questions • Paper or poster board, one per participant • Markers, for class to share • Poster of "Interview Questions"	• Set out poster board. • Set out markers. • Select four to six interview questions. • Post shield examples on the wall.
Session 5: Getting Acquainted	Through activities and discussion, participants develop relationships beyond just a surface level and build conversation skills.	• 8½" x 11" paper, one per participant • Pens or pencils, one per participant	• Set out paper. • Set out pens or pencils.
Session 6: Building a Neighborhood	Through creation of neighborhoods from basic materials, participants will learn how to work together toward a common goal.	• Poster board, one per every five to six participants • Various materials, such as construction paper, markers, toilet paper rolls, Popsicle sticks, and pipe cleaners	• Set out pieces of poster board. • Set out materials.

BUILDING ASSETS, REDUCING RISKS

Duplicating this page is illegal. Do not duplicate without publisher's written permission.

17

Session 1: House Rules

TIME NEEDED

- 30 minutes

ASSET CATEGORIES

- Boundaries and Expectations
- Empowerment
- Commitment to Learning

RISK/PROTECTIVE FACTORS

- Bonding and attachment to school

MATERIALS NEEDED

- Whiteboard or Smart Board
- Markers
- Poster board, three to five pieces

PREPARATION NEEDED

- No preparation is needed.

Purpose

To establish rules for creating a respectful community within the classroom

Instructions

1. Explain I-Time:

   - Explain the purpose of I-Time as building relationships, having fun, learning about good communication, setting goals, taking care of yourself, recognizing diversity in our school, and other topics.

   - Provide an overview of the topics that will be addressed and the schedule of activities.

   - Emphasize that everyone (participants as well as the facilitator) participates in I-Time: Participation is an important part of the class.

2. Establish house rules:

   - Explain what you mean by "house rules."

   - Ask participants why house rules are important in a classroom. Be sure the discussion mentions the need to foster a caring and respectful environment. (This conversation encourages participants to examine their own ideas and determine the importance of rules themselves; it is a meaningful activity for the group.)

   - Ask all participants to work in a large group and brainstorm ideas for house rules for the class. Record all responses on the whiteboard or Smart Board.

   - Prepare participants to vote on the house rules. Ask participants why it is important to vote on the rules (for example, the need for consensus; agreement to follow the rules).

- Ask participants if the class suggestions are rules they can live with. Participants may discuss and edit the list of brainstormed rules if needed.

- Ask participants to vote on the house rules. Voting yes means participants agree to follow these rules.

- Agree to add rules throughout the school year as needed.

- Have participants write the house rules on three pieces of poster board and post the rules in a visible place in the three block classrooms. If you have a support block with four block facilitators, create four posters.

3. Each class develops its own house rules. Here are some sample rules:

- Speak for yourself—not everyone else.

- Listen to others and they will listen to you.

- Avoid put-downs.

- Show respect.

- Keep discussions confidential. (Some I-Time sessions are self-revealing; confidentiality should be explained and agreed to by the entire class: "What is said here, stays here.")

- One person talks at a time; no side conversations.

Facilitator note: Inform participants that if they share information about someone harming them or about their plans to harm themselves or others, the facilitator is legally required to report this. Let participants know this ahead of time, so they aren't surprised later.

Optional Follow-Up

Revisit this activity when class "house rules" are broken. Rules can be added as necessary throughout the year.

Grades 6–8 Adaptations

No adaptations are needed.

Session 2: "Do You Know Your Neighbor?"

TIME NEEDED

- 15 minutes

ASSET CATEGORIES

- Commitment to Learning
- Social Competencies
- Support

RISK/PROTECTIVE FACTORS

- Bonding and attachment to school

MATERIALS NEEDED

- Chairs, one chair per participant minus one

PREPARATION NEEDED

- Place chairs in a circle.

Purpose

To build community in the classroom by learning participants' names and anecdotal information about each other

Instructions

1. Place the chairs in a circle, facing inward.

2. Have all participants sit down except for one individual who stands inside the circle of chairs.

3. This game is a variation of musical chairs. The person standing inside the circle selects one participant and asks, "Do you know your neighbor?" The person who was asked the question responds by introducing the people sitting on both sides of her. If the participant doesn't know their names, she asks each person's name and then introduces her neighbors to the group.

4. The person standing then asks the same participant, "Who else would you like to know?" and the participant calls out a criterion for everyone in the group (such as "I want to know who is wearing blue jeans"). All participants who meet this criterion stand up and move to new chairs at least two chairs away. The participant who was standing in the middle of the circle also finds a chair. A participant who didn't find a chair and is left standing moves to the middle and asks another participant, "Do you know your neighbor?" and the process is repeated.

5. Urge participants to be creative when they call out criteria. Here are some sample criteria:

   - Physical characteristics: everyone who wears glasses or contacts, everyone who has brown hair, or everyone who has black socks on

- Family traits: everyone who has a brother, everyone with a grandparent who is alive, or everyone who has lived in another state

- Hobbies or experiences: everyone who has traveled out of the country or everyone who has a job

- Any other criteria that would apply to participants, such as favorite foods or owning pets

6. Have fun safely!

Optional Follow-Up

Use the questions from this exercise (such as "Who was born in another state?" or "Who has an older brother?") as a method to determine partners or groups for future projects.

Grades 6–8 Adaptations

Display sample questions so all participants can see them. Suggest that participants pick one of the questions displayed or create their own.

BUILDING ASSETS, REDUCING RISKS

Duplicating this page is illegal. Do not duplicate without publisher's written permission.

21

Session 3: Commonalities

TIME NEEDED

- 20 minutes

ASSET CATEGORIES

- Support
- Constructive Use of Time

RISK/PROTECTIVE FACTORS

- Bonding and attachment to school

MATERIALS NEEDED

- Commonalities handout
- Pens or pencils, one per participant

PREPARATION NEEDED

- Print and copy the Commonalities handout, one per participant.

Purpose

To help participants learn about each other and their commonalities

Instructions

1. Have participants partner up with someone they do not know very well.

2. Distribute the Commonalities handout and the pens or pencils.

3. Ask participants to talk with their partner and find at least five areas they have in common (for example, they both love pizza or both have a dog). Participants should use the handout as a guide and write their commonalities on the handout. Allow ten minutes for discussion.

4. If time allows, ask participants to share their commonalities with the larger group.

▶ Facilitator note: Add additional areas to fit the needs, characteristics, and interests of your class.

Optional Follow-Up

This activity could be repeated later in the year with participants selecting new partners.

Grades 6–8 Adaptations

No adaptations are needed.

BUILDING ASSETS, REDUCING RISKS

Commonalities

Try to find at least five things you have in common with your partner.

AREAS TO EXPLORE ▼

Where you were born: _____

Childhood experience: _____

_____

_____

Family situation: _____

_____

Sports (you enjoy or participate in): _____

Music (you enjoy or participate in): _____

Favorite foods: _____

Vacations: _____

Movies: _____

Pet peeves: _____

Hobbies: _____

Books: _____

Pets: _____

Jobs you've had: _____

_____

1 of 1

Session 4: Shields

TIME NEEDED

• 1 hour

ASSET CATEGORIES

• Support
• Positive Identity
• Commitment to Learning

RISK/PROTECTIVE FACTORS

• Bonding and attachment to school
• Opportunities for pro-social involvement

MATERIALS NEEDED

• Paper or poster board, one piece per participant
• Markers, enough for the class to share

PREPARATION NEEDED

• Select four to six questions from the Shield Interview Questions list (found after this session outline) and write them on the whiteboard or Smart Board
• Optional: Prepare some examples of shields.
• Optional: Create stencils so participants can easily trace the outline of the shield onto their paper or poster board.

Purpose

To help participants become more acquainted with one another and introduce each other to the entire class

Instructions

1. Prior to class, select four to six interview questions for participants to use from the Shield Interview Questions list (see page 27). They will use these questions to create a shield about someone else in the class.

2. Give each participant a sheet of paper or poster board. Instruct participants to draw the outline of a shield on their paper, dividing the shield into sections (four to six sections based on the number of questions the facilitator provides).

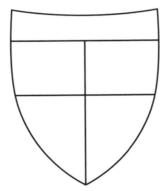 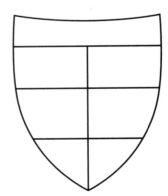

3. Explain that each participant is going to make a shield and a coat of arms/family crest on this sheet of paper or poster board. Talk about the long tradition behind these elements:

   • As far back as the twelfth century, shields were taken into battle in France and other areas of Europe for identification purposes. When knights were wearing armor, it was difficult to tell who was who. The elements on the shield allowed other knights to know the wearer's allegiances and military status.

- The coat of arms/crest on the shield was a symbol or logo that signified something about the person. This might be one or more animals, an image such as an anchor, or something other-worldly, such as an angel.

- The color of the shield also represented characteristics of the knight. For example, red might represent bold-ness and green might symbolize ambition.

Although they are no longer worn by armored knights, we still see coats of arms/crests today. Family coats of arms/ crests may be handed down through the generations and convey something about a person's ancestors; crests are also used by some schools and colleges, organizations, or even businesses.

4. Instruct participants to find a partner they don't know very well. All participants, including the facilitator, work with a partner to create shields and coats of arms/crests.

5. Partners will take turns interviewing each other using the shield questions.

- Each participant writes her or his partner's name on the top of the shield.

- Partners interview each other asking the shield questions provided by the facilitator.

- Each participant writes or draws answers to her or his partner's questions in a section on the shield.

6. When the interviews are completed, have participants introduce their partners to the class by sharing infor-mation from the interview and using the shield as a visual aid.

Optional Follow-Up

After all participants have introduced their partner, store the shields until a future time (such as the last day of the quarter or the end of the semester). Then hang the shields around the room and have all participants write positive comments about the person on her or his shield. Allow the participants to take the shields home after the positive comments have been added.

Grades 6–8 Adaptations

- Display sample shields for participants to see ideas of images and symbols used in real shields.

- Set out stencils of various shapes and pictures of various objects so participants can use them to draw their shields.

- Simplify the language for step 3, for example: Coats of arms/ crests and shields have been used since the 1100s in England and France. The colors, figures, and symbols all represent something about the person or the person's family.

BUILDING ASSETS, REDUCING RISKS

26   Duplicating this page is illegal. Do not duplicate without publisher's written permission.

Shield Interview Questions

Choose four to six questions from the following list for use with session 4.

1. If you could travel anywhere in the world, where would you go?

2. What famous person would you most like to meet and what would you talk about with him or her?

3. What one person has had the biggest influence on your life and why?

4. Describe what your ideal summer would be.

5. What are the qualities your friends say they like about you?

6. What is the best movie you've ever seen and what did you like most about it?

7. Who is your hero and why?

8. What is your greatest accomplishment?

9. What is the happiest event of your life?

10. What is one thing about school you like?

11. If you could win a gold medal in the Olympics, what event would you choose?

BUILDING ASSETS, REDUCING RISKS

Duplicating this page is illegal. Do not duplicate without publisher's written permission.

27

Session 5: Getting Acquainted

TIME NEEDED

• 30 minutes

ASSET CATEGORIES

• Support
• Social Competencies

RISK/PROTECTIVE FACTORS

• Bonding and attachment to school
• Increase in social skills

MATERIALS NEEDED

• 8½" x 11" paper, one sheet per participant
• Pens or pencils, one per participant

PREPARATION NEEDED

• Set out paper.
• Set out pens or pencils.

Purpose

To provide an opportunity for participants and staff to develop relationships beyond just a surface level and to build conversation skills

Instructions

1. Instruct participants to each take one sheet of paper and draw lines, dividing the paper into six equal sections.

2. Ask participants to write a letter in each section (a–f).

3. Ask participants to answer each question in the corresponding section of their papers (a–f):

   a. What was your favorite toy as a child?

   b. If you could go to any concert, what concert would you attend? Whom would you invite to go with you?

   c. What is your favorite memory as a child (for example, family time, birthday party, time with a neighbor)?

   d. Who are two teachers you are glad you had (such as schoolteacher, faith-based teacher, Girl Scout/Boy Scout leader, or piano or musical instrument teacher)?

   e. What is your favorite comfort food?

   f. Draw a picture of yourself at work in your dream job fifteen to twenty years from now. What are you doing?

4. Ask participants to choose a partner they do not know very well and to share one or two of their answers with each other. Suggest that each partner talks for three minutes and then they alternate who is speaking.

5. Find new partners and share again, as time allows.

Optional Follow-Up

Save participants' sheets and use the information (such as favorite concert or comfort food) when engaging them in conversation throughout the year.

Grades 6–8 Adaptations

No adaptations are needed.

BUILDING ASSETS, REDUCING RISKS

Duplicating this page is illegal. Do not duplicate without publisher's written permission.

29

Session 6: Building a Neighborhood

TIME NEEDED

• At least 1 hour

ASSET CATEGORIES

• Social Competencies
• Support

RISK/PROTECTIVE FACTORS

• Bonding and attachment to school

MATERIALS NEEDED

• Poster board, one piece for every five to six participants
• Various materials that can be used to build a model neighborhood, such as construction paper, markers, toilet paper rolls, Popsicle sticks, and pipe cleaners

PREPARATION NEEDED

• No preparation is needed other than gathering supplies and setting them out.

Purpose

To learn that an effective team requires individuals to assume various roles

Instructions

1. Divide the class into groups (five to six participants per group).

2. Ask each group to discuss this question: "If you could build an ideal neighborhood, what would be in that neighborhood?" Allow ten minutes for discussion, encouraging group members to arrive at a consensus in that time period.

3. Inform participants that each group will be building their ideal neighborhood using a piece of poster board as a base and various materials. Each group will need to use members' creativity to build their ideal neighborhood.

4. When finished, each group will present its ideal neighborhood to the class. Participants in other groups will then have the opportunity to ask questions and provide feedback to the presenting group.

5. Following the neighborhood group presentations, lead a discussion using the following questions:

   • What methods were used to build the neighborhoods?
   • Were there one or more persons in charge?
   • How were decisions made?
   • Were there disagreements? If so, how were disagreements handled?
   • Did your group reach a consensus?

- Are there similarities between this neighborhood-building team experience and other team experiences in life? Any differences?

- How did your group identify the factors that make a neighborhood ideal?

- What roles do you think are necessary for a group to work effectively?

Optional Follow-Up

Remind the class of this activity and the skills necessary to work effectively as a team when assigning group projects later in the school year.

Grades 6–8 Adaptations

- Show pictures of simple neighborhoods that participants can use as models for the neighborhoods they create (for example, show sample houses, apartments, parks, or stores), or as a whole class briefly discuss what makes up a neighborhood before participants break into their groups.

- Simplify the questions for step 5:

  - How did you build the neighborhood?

  - Were there one or more persons in charge?

  - What did the rest of the team members do? Did they have specific roles?

  - Did you agree all of the time?

  - If not, how did you settle the disagreement?

  - What did you agree on?

  - What other teams have you worked on? (For example, working with siblings to complete chores or athletic teams)

BUILDING ASSETS, REDUCING RISKS

Duplicating this page is illegal. Do not duplicate without publisher's written permission.

31

Section 2: Goals

Session Title	Session Description	Materials Needed	Preparation Needed
Session 7: Crossing the River	Through helping their teammates "cross the river," participants learn a process for establishing and reaching a goal.	• 8½" x 11" paper, forty-eight sheets	• Print and copy the Master Grid for Crossing the River document, one per small group. • Mark a path on each master grid from the first row to the last row, making the path different on each grid. • Arrange sheets of paper on the floor.
Session 8: Person of the Year	Through discussion of values and wisdom, participants identify the need for goals and dreams.	• Person of the Year handout • Pens or pencils, one per participant	• Print and copy Person of the Year handout, one per participant.
Session 9: Personal Goal-Setting	Through completion of the various handouts, participants begin to set their own personal goals.	• Personal Goals handout • Goal Tree Example handout • Your Personal Goal Tree handout • Pens or pencils, one per participant	• Print and copy Personal Goals, Goal Tree Example, and Your Personal Goal Tree handouts, one per participant.
Session 10: Decision-Making	Through completion of handouts and small group discussions, participants understand and practice a decision-making process.	• ABCDE Decision-Making Model handout • Decision-Making handout	• Print and copy the ABCDE Decision-Making Model and Decision-Making handouts, one per participant.

BUILDING ASSETS, REDUCING RISKS

Duplicating this page is illegal. Do not duplicate without publisher's written permission.

33

Session 7: Crossing the River

Purpose

To learn a process for establishing and reaching a goal

Additional Preparation

On each copy of the master grid, mark a path from one side to the other using numbers. An example is shown below. The squares, or "stones," in each path do not necessarily need to be adjacent but arranged so that a participant would be able to step from one stone to the next and safely cross the river. There should be at least one stone (number) in each row. Each group should have a different path. Do not show participants the master grids.

Sample Master Grid

On the classroom floor, arrange sheets of paper in eight rows and six columns (or forty-eight pieces of paper total) similar to the grid below.

Start

		1			
				2	3	
						4
				6		5
			7			
		8				
	9					
		10				

Finish

Instructions

1. Explain that the goal of this activity is for one participant from each team to safely cross an imaginary river. One team works on crossing the river at a time until someone on the team succeeds; then another team has a turn. Team members take turns trying to find the rocks in the river to step on, across all eight rows of stones to the shore, or the finish.

2. Have participants form teams of four to six people. Explain that the six-by-eight grid of papers in front of them is the "river" and that there are rocks hidden below the surface that they must step on to cross the river. Each team works together to guide one team member safely across the river.

3. The first participant on a team steps on a sheet of paper in the first row of the river. The facilitator refers to the master grid with the path of rocks marked. If the master grid shows that piece of paper is not a rock, the participant is told that he or she has fallen in the river. The person's turn is over, and he or she returns to the end of the team line.

4. A second participant from the same team then tries standing on another sheet of paper in the first row, seeking the rocks to safely cross the river, and the facilitator refers to the master grid to determine if that paper is a rock. If a participant successfully finds a rock, he or she then chooses another piece of paper to step on to find the next rock in the path. If it is not a rock, that person's turn is over.

5. Participants continue to try to find the rocks that make the path to cross the river. All class members can observe, but only team members can help guide the person across the river by remembering which papers have already been found to be rocks. Team members can coach the person on where the safe spots are by saying "left," "right," or "straight" to help their team member cross the river.

BUILDING ASSETS, REDUCING RISKS
Duplicating this page is illegal. Do not duplicate without publisher's written permission.

35

6. Once a team member has successfully crossed the river, that team's turn is done. The facilitator uses a different grid of stones and the process begins again with a new team, playing for as long as time allows. After the game is completed, the facilitator leads a group discussion using the following questions:

Part One

- How did it feel to have your team members watch your attempt to cross the river?

- What was most helpful in crossing the river?

- Were there some risks involved in crossing the river?

Part Two

- Each person's goal in the game was to cross the river safely, despite the risks. Are there risks involved in reaching personal goals?

- How does the support of teammates help in achieving your goals?

- How does this activity relate to goal setting (for example, have others go before you, get advice on safe spots and pitfalls, or give each other encouragement)?

Optional Follow-Up

During times when participants are struggling to reach their goals, remind them of the Crossing the River activity. Use questions such as

- What do you recall about being a member of a team?

- Who are the rocks in your lives (parent[s]/guardian[s], grandparent[s], relatives, friends, or a favorite teacher/ facilitator or coach)?

- What qualities about that person make him or her a rock?

NOTES

BUILDING ASSETS, REDUCING RISKS

36

Duplicating this page is illegal. Do not duplicate without publisher's written permission.

- How does this person show you support?

- How can you be a support to others?

Grades 6–8 Adaptations

- Simplify the questions for part 2:

  – What was the goal for this activity?

  – What did you need to do to reach the goal?

  – How did your teammates help you reach your goal?

BUILDING ASSETS, REDUCING RISKS

Duplicating this page is illegal. Do not duplicate without publisher's written permission.

37

Master Grid for
Crossing the River

Mark a path across the river, using numbers to indicate where each safe "rock" is located. There should be at least one number per row. Not all numbers need to be adjacent, but participants will need to be able to easily step from one stone to another. Each small group will need a different master grid.

Start

Finish

BUILDING ASSETS, REDUCING RISKS

Session 8: Person of the Year

TIME NEEDED

- 30 minutes

ASSET CATEGORIES

- Positive Values
- Social Competencies
- Positive Identity

RISK/PROTECTIVE FACTORS

- Leadership and decision-making opportunities
- Developing positive future plans

MATERIALS NEEDED

- Person of the Year handout 8-1
- Pens or pencils, one per participant

PREPARATION NEEDED

- Print and copy the Person of the Year handout, one per participant.

Purpose

To demonstrate the need for goals and dreams

Instructions

1. Distribute the Person of the Year handout and a pen or pencil to each participant.

2. Have each person complete the handout individually.

3. Ask participants to find partners and share their answers.

4. Reconvene as a large group and ask each pair to share as many responses as time allows.

5. Discuss the following questions with the group:

   - What goals do you think the Person of the Year set to achieve his or her success?

   - What has made this person successful? (Differing opinions will be voiced; acknowledge each person's opinion and stress there are no wrong answers.)

   - Are there differing opinions on what is success?

   - What kind of leadership has this person shown?

   - What kinds of decisions do you think this person has made to be recognized and appear on the magazine cover?

Optional Follow-Up

At various intervals during the school year, discuss individuals who appear on magazine covers.

BUILDING ASSETS, REDUCING RISKS

Duplicating this page is illegal. Do not duplicate without publisher's written permission.

39

Grades 6–8 Adaptations

- Give a sample answer for every question on the Person of the Year handout, so participants better understand how to answer the questions.

- Simplify the questions in step 5:

  - What goals do you think the Person of the Year had?

  - What do you think the person did to reach these goals? What steps did he or she likely take?

  - Is this person successful? Why?

Person of the Year

It is twenty years from now and you have been chosen as the "Person of the Year." Your portrait will grace the cover of many magazines and your life story will be featured in many issues. You need to complete the following questionnaire for the writer to begin her or his article on you. Please answer to the best of your ability all the questions that apply.

Given name: _____

Date of birth: _____

Place of birth: _____

Family members: _____

Pet(s): _____

Interests/hobbies: _____

What accomplishments would you like to be remembered for?

_____

_____

What are three values that are important to you?

_____

_____

Name the most influential person in your life and how he or she has influenced you:

_____

_____

Words of wisdom to live by: _____

Now imagine that this honor has come to you at a time in your life when you have accomplished your life work. What are you being recognized for?

_____

_____

1 of 1

Session 9: Personal Goal-Setting

TIME NEEDED

• 30 minutes

ASSET CATEGORIES

• Social Competencies
• Positive Identity

RISK/PROTECTIVE FACTORS

• Leadership and decision-making opportunities
• Developing positive future plans

MATERIALS NEEDED

• Personal Goals handout
• Goal Tree Example handout
• Your Personal Goal Tree handout
• Pens or pencils, one per participant

PREPARATION NEEDED

• Print and copy the three handouts, one copy per participant.

Purpose

To set personal goals

Instructions

1. Distribute the Personal Goals handout and a pen or pencil to each participant.

2. Have each person complete the handout individually.

3. Distribute the Goal Tree Example handout. Using the Goal Tree directions, explain the process of developing goals using the Goal Tree as a guide.

4. Distribute the Your Personal Goal Tree handout and have participants individually identify and write their personal goals on the handout.

5. If time allows, have participants share their goals with the whole group or with another person.

Optional Follow-Up

• Use the Personal Goals handout and the Your Personal Goal Tree handout for parent/guardian conferences.

• Review these handouts periodically during the year with participants. Ask participants to reflect on their answers to the Personal Goals handout, the Your Personal Goal Tree handout, and answer these questions:

  – Are there any surprises—things you didn't remember were your goals?

  – Are your goals still a fit? Would you change any of your goals?

  – What has occurred that would cause you to change your personal goals? (Participants should share based on their comfort level.)

Grades 6–8 Adaptations

Show the participants a completed Your Personal Goal Tree handout, so they better understand how to fill one out.

Personal Goals

Describe some of your personal goals below.

By the end of the day, I plan to _____

_____

By the end of the week, I plan to _____

_____

By the end of the year, I plan to _____

_____

During the summer, I plan to _____

_____

After finishing high school, I plan to _____

_____

A place I plan to visit is _____

The one thing I would like to change about myself is _____

_____

_____

In ten years, my career will be _____

_____

BUILDING ASSETS, REDUCING RISKS

Goal Tree Example

When writing goals, it is very important to be specific about what you intend to accomplish. Using a Goal Tree is one way to narrow down the things you'd like to accomplish. An example is provided. Review it carefully from the bottom up. Use this example as a guide when completing your personal Goal Tree.

Be even more specific.

1. Get better grades

2. Enjoy classes more

3. Spend more time studying

Name three ways you could accomplish it.

Do better in school

State a goal.

Your Personal Goal Tree

Complete your personal Goal Tree. Consider the following when determining goals:

1. **Conceivable**—Can I put it into words?
2. **Believable**—Does it fit me?
3. **Achievable**—Can I accomplish it?
4. **Controllable**—Can I control it?

5. **Measurable**—Can I measure it?
6. **Desirable**—Do I really want to do it?
7. **Stated with no alternative**—I will do it.

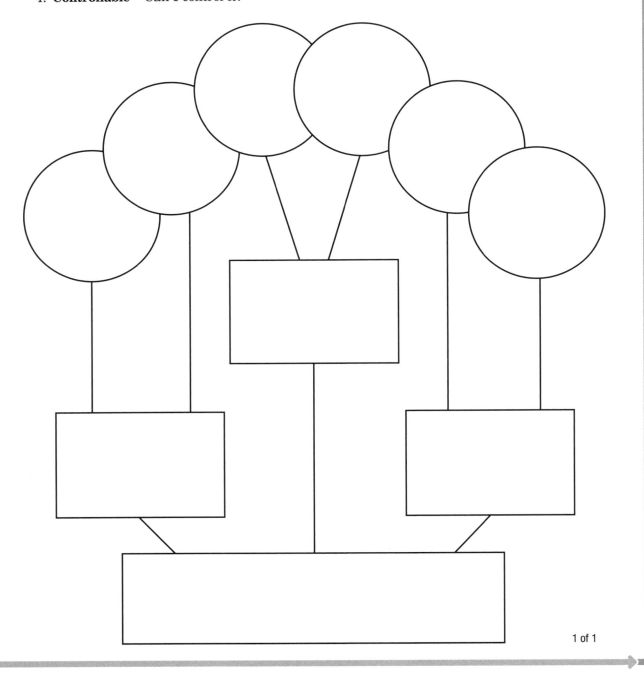

1 of 1

Session 10: Decision-Making

TIME NEEDED

- 30 minutes

ASSET CATEGORIES

- Social Competencies
- Positive Identity

RISK/PROTECTIVE FACTORS

- Leadership and decision-making opportunities
- Developing positive future plans

MATERIALS NEEDED

- ABCDE Decision-Making Model handout 10-1
- Decision-Making handout 10-2
- Pens or pencils, one per participant

PREPARATION NEEDED

- Print and copy the two handouts, one copy per participant.

Purpose

To understand and practice a decision-making process

Instructions

1. Distribute the ABCDE Decision-Making Model handout to each participant.

2. Ask the participants to think of a time when they needed to make a decision and how they made that decision.

3. Explain that today's session will focus on a process that can be used to make decisions. Review the ABCDE Decision-Making Model handout with participants.

4. Distribute the Decision-Making handout and a pen or pencil. Ask participants to complete the handout individually, thinking of a present, past, or near future situation. Sample situations for the Decision-Making handout may include

   - choosing classes for next year

   - deciding whether to join a sport or activity

   - deciding whether to use or refuse alcohol or other drugs

   - deciding whether to break off a friendship

5. Divide the class into small groups (two to three participants per group). Have participants share the decision and decision-making steps they wrote about on the handout with their small group and ask group members to offer feedback. After each participant has had time to share with his or her small group, bring the whole class together and discuss the following questions:

   - What are your thoughts about this decision-making model?

   - Is it easy to use?

BUILDING ASSETS, REDUCING RISKS

Duplicating this page is illegal. Do not duplicate without publisher's written permission.

47

- Were there parts of the model that were very helpful? Somewhat helpful?

- What was the most helpful feedback you received from the other members of your group?

- How do feedback and support from peers help in making decisions?

Optional Follow-Up

Remind participants to think about this process when they need to make decisions.

Grades 6–8 Adaptations

No adaptations are needed.

BUILDING ASSETS, REDUCING RISKS

48   Duplicating this page is illegal. Do not duplicate without publisher's written permission.

ABCDE Decision-Making Model

Below is a model for making decisions. Read over the process and then think about a time when you needed to make a decision and how you made that decision.

A = Aware

Identify the decision.

- What decision do I have to make?

B = Brainstorm

Generate a list of all possibilities.

- What are my choices?
- Think of all the possible options.

C = Consequences and Choose

Identify the consequences of each option and choose the best.

- If I make this choice, what will happen?
- Which option offers the most positive consequences?
- Choose the most beneficial.

D = Deliver

Put your choice into action.

- Follow through; act on your decision.
- Deliver the goods.

E = Examine

- Was this the best choice for me?
- Did it work out?
- Should I do it differently next time?

Source: Office of Safety Programs. "Juvenile Alternative Sentencing Program: A Substance Abuse Education Program." Charleston, IL: Eastern Illinois University, 1989.

1 of 1

Decision-Making

Think of a decision you are currently facing, one you have faced in the past, or one you will be faced with in the near future. Then answer the following questions about your decision-making process.

1. What are the possible options for this decision?

_____

_____

2. List the positives of each option.

_____

_____

3. List the negatives of each option.

_____

_____

4. What decision would you make right now?

_____

_____

5. Ask someone else about the situation. What does he or she recommend?

_____

_____

6. Would you make the same decision now after receiving feedback?

_____

_____

7. Who could you consult with and ask for feedback when you have an important decision to make in your life?

_____

_____

BUILDING ASSETS, REDUCING RISKS

Section 3: Leadership

Session Title	Session Description	Materials Needed	Preparation Needed
Session 11: Leadership Style	Through brainstorming, completing handouts, and discussion, participants define their own leadership style.	• Leadership Packet • Whiteboard or Smart Board • Markers • Pens or pencils, one per participant	• Print and copy Leadership Packet, one per participant.
Session 12: Straw Towers and Create a Game	Through constructing a straw tower and creating a game from found objects, participants discover how to work with others who have similar and different leadership styles.	• Straws, twenty for every six to eight participants • Masking tape • Box of various materials, such as balls, paper cups, rubber binders, spoons, string, or paper plates	• Cut off 25" strips of tape, one per group of six to eight participants. • Set out the box of materials.

BUILDING ASSETS, REDUCING RISKS

Duplicating this page is illegal. Do not duplicate without publisher's written permission.

51

Session 11: Leadership Style

TIME NEEDED

• 30 minutes

ASSET CATEGORIES

• Positive Identity
• Social Competencies

RISK/PROTECTIVE FACTORS

• Leadership and decision-making opportunities

MATERIALS NEEDED

• Leadership Packet [11-1]
• Whiteboard or Smart Board
• Markers
• Pens or pencils, one per participant

PREPARATION NEEDED

• Print and copy the Leadership Packet, one per participant.

Purpose

To help participants define their own leadership style

Instructions

1. Ask all participants to brainstorm the following questions. Write the responses on a whiteboard or Smart Board.

   • What is a leader?

   • What qualities are important in a leader?

   • What qualities are needed to show leadership?

2. Continue the discussion by asking the large group the following question. Record all responses on the whiteboard or Smart Board.

   • Do you think leaders have different styles?

3. Distribute the Leadership Packet and pens or pencils, asking all participants to complete the Behavioral Characteristics Rating Form.

4. Ask participants to self-score their survey answers on the Behavioral Characteristics Score Sheet. Explain:

   • The number circled for number one on the Behavioral Characteristics Rating Form would be placed in the first column next to the number one on the Behavioral Characteristics Score Sheet. Continue with the rest of the questions. Add up each column and complete the formula to receive a score.

5. Ask participants to locate their leadership style on the Behavioral Matrix. Read the descriptions of leadership styles found in the Leadership Packet.

6. Discuss leadership styles by asking the following questions:

- How did you feel when you read about your leadership style? How do you feel about your rating? Is it a fit for you? Were there any surprises?

- How can learning about leadership styles help us in everyday life?

Optional Follow-Up

Ask participants to think about and discuss the leadership styles of leaders in our world, past and present.

Grades 6–8 Adaptations

No adaptations are needed.

Leadership Packet

Name _____

Behavioral Characteristics Rating Form

Directions: Circle the numbers to indicate how you rate yourself on the following characteristics.

1.	Appears confident	1	2	3	4	Insecure
2.	Passive	1	2	3	4	Aggressive
3.	Reactive	1	2	3	4	Self-controlled
4.	Easygoing	1	2	3	4	Dominant
5.	Takes charge	1	2	3	4	Goes along
6.	Formal	1	2	3	4	Informal
7.	Disciplined	1	2	3	4	Spontaneous
8.	Communicates easily	1	2	3	4	Hesitant communicator
9.	Accepting	1	2	3	4	Challenging
10.	Appears unorganized	1	2	3	4	Appears organized
11.	Initiates social contact	1	2	3	4	Lets others initiate
12.	Asks questions	1	2	3	4	Makes statements
13.	Overbearing	1	2	3	4	Shy
14.	Reserved	1	2	3	4	Fun loving
15.	Appears active	1	2	3	4	Appears thoughtful
16.	Relaxed	1	2	3	4	Assertive
17.	Withholds feelings	1	2	3	4	Expresses feelings
18.	Relationship oriented	1	2	3	4	Task oriented
19.	Pushy	1	2	3	4	Gentle
20.	Discriminating	1	2	3	4	Impulsive
21.	Extrovert	1	2	3	4	Introvert
22.	Warm	1	2	3	4	Cool
23.	Subtle	1	2	3	4	Direct
24.	Distant	1	2	3	4	Close
25.	States information	1	2	3	4	Saves information
26.	Quiet	1	2	3	4	Talkative

1 of 8

Behavioral Characteristics Score Sheet

To locate your style on the Dominant/ Easygoing Scale, place the numbers you circled on the Behavioral Characteristics Rating Form on the line following the corresponding question numbers below:

1. _____   2. _____

5. _____   4. _____

8. _____   9. _____

11. _____   12. _____

13. _____   16. _____

15. _____   23. _____

19. _____   26. _____

21. _____

25. _____

Sum #1 _____   Sum #2 _____

(Sum #1) + 35   = _____
                     (Total 1)

(Total 1) – (Sum #2) = _____
                          (Total 2)

(Total 2) ÷ 16   = _____

Place an X on the following scale corresponding to the score above:

Dominant _____ Easy-Going
         1   2   3   4

To locate your style on the Formal/ Informal Scale, place the numbers you circled on the Behavioral Characteristics Rating Form on the line following the corresponding question numbers below:

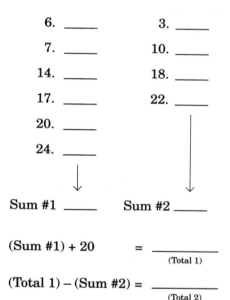

6. _____   3. _____

7. _____   10. _____

14. _____   18. _____

17. _____   22. _____

20. _____

24. _____

Sum #1 _____   Sum #2 _____

(Sum #1) + 20   = _____
                     (Total 1)

(Total 1) – (Sum #2) = _____
                          (Total 2)

(Total 2) ÷ 10   = _____

Place an X on the following scale corresponding to the score above:

Formal _____ Informal
       1   2   3   4

2 of 8

55

The Behavioral Matrix: A Brief Description

Psychologists describe behavior as a function of perception. The feelings, beliefs, conditions, attitudes, and understandings of a person constitute the directing forces of her or his behavior.

Because people have complex and overlapping values and beliefs, it is impossible to describe a person as having a specific, unalterable behavioral style. However, some opposite behavior patterns can be recognized that operate on a vertical continuum of informal and formal, and on a horizontal dimension of dominant and easy-going. The intersection of these opposites forms four quadrants that can be said to represent four broad categories of behavior style: the promoter, supporter, controller, and analyzer.

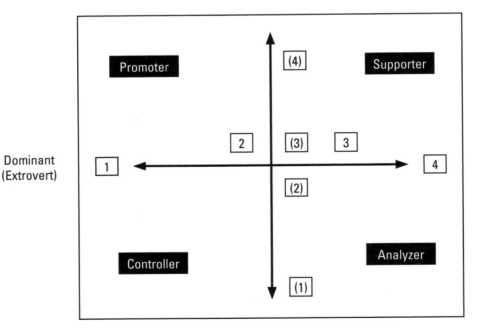

BUILDING ASSETS, REDUCING RISKS

Productive and Excessive Characteristics
of Each Behavioral Style

INFORMAL

DOMINANT

Promoter

- inconsistent	+ flexible
- childlike	+ youthful
- agitated	+ enthusiastic
- afraid of confrontation	+ tactful
- lacking in conviction	+ socially skillful
- manipulative	

Supporter

- impractical	+ idealistic
- gullible	+ trusting
- paternalistic	+ helpful
- passive	+ receptive
- self-deprecating	+ modest
- obligated	+ loyal
- perfectionist	+ aspiring

EASY-GOING

Controller

- domineering	+ controlling
- impulsive	+ quick to act
- arrogant	+ self-confident
- coercive	+ forceful
- high pressure	+ persistent
- impatient	+ urgent
- unstable	+ eager to change

Analyzer

- dull	+ practical
- stingy	+ economical
- unfriendly	+ reserved
- compulsive	+ thorough
- plodding	+ methodical
- critical	+ analytical
- stubborn	+ steadfast

FORMAL

Each Behavioral Style Will Excel in a Situation Where . . .

Promoter

- People are involved (such as committee work).

- New possibilities need to be brainstormed.

- There is a defined structure with boundaries.

- Follow-through is forced by someone else.

- Inspirations are allowed and encouraged.

- There is a lot of attention (they'll take anything, including negative put-downs).

- They can talk about what is learned (for example, tons of discussion).

- There is action-oriented activity (such as role playing, drama, learning multiplication tables by jumping rope at the same time).

- The environment is optimistic, changing.

- They are surrounded by friendliness and warmth.

Controller

- Organized information abounds and is valued.

- They are allowed to take responsibility and leadership.

- The environment is fast moving and challenging.

- There is a chance to assume a leadership role.

- Competition abounds.

- There is freedom to accomplish tasks their own way.

- There is an established authority to respect.

- Academic achievement is highly valued.

continued on next page

Supporter

- They can please others.

- Harmony, respect, and good feelings exist.

- Research and learning is about people.

- Structure, supervision, and guidance are available.

- There is much reassurance, support, and personal attention.

- Ideas can be developed that will benefit others.

- Relationship skills can be applied to get the job done (such as through committee work).

- They can give and give and give.

- The environment is idealistic.

- Their loyalty is valued.

Analyzer

- They can work by themselves.

- The environment is unemotional, factual, and practical.

- There is freedom to ponder.

- The leader gives a systematic, structured framework.

- Routine is the watchword.

- There is a lack of pressure—low-key.

- Much attention is given for task results.

- Value is placed on accumulation of facts.

- They can save face even when they may be wrong.

- There are rules for dealing with others.

Conflicts Typical of Each Behavioral Style

Promoter

- Others may feel steamrolled.

- Rapid change causes others to see action as shotgunning and unstable.

- Excitement may be seen as egotism.

- Forceful, aggressive, up-front nature may cause others to see trait as manipulative.

- Impatience can result in arguments.

Controller

- Efforts to get tasks accomplished may make others feel run over.

- Any idle bystander will be included when organizing the situation.

- Hearing others tell them what and how to get the task done will lead to backup on completing tasks.

- Anger and impatience moves quickly when distracted by the promoter's spontaneity.

- Critical and judgmental eye will create distance with others.

Supporter

- Logic fails to move viewpoint, creating impatience with analyzers and controllers.

- Sensitivity leads to resentment over what is perceived as tactlessness of others; assumes others are there too.

- Harmony is valued over anything else and agreement is preferred.

- Own interests are subordinate to those of others.

- Unpleasant information is withheld.

continued on next page

Analyzer

- Serious, orderly manner draws impatience from others.

- Critical and judgmental eye toward others creates distancing.

- Indecisions create confusion and impatience.

- When cornered, pressure builds quickly.

- Allowing others to initiate may build resentment over time.

- States position bluntly, without concern and feeling for others.

- Feels rejected unless a group is willing to draw out data and warmth.

Session 12: Straw Towers and Create a Game

- 30–60 minutes

- Social Competencies
- Positive Identity
- Support

- Opportunities for pro-social involvement

- Straws, twenty per group of six to eight participants
- Masking tape
- A box of various materials, such as balls, paper cups, rubber binders, spoons, string, or paper plates. Have enough items so each group can have two or three different items.

- Set out the box of materials.
- Cut the masking tape into 25" pieces, one piece per group of six to eight participants.

Purpose

To discover how to work with people who have similar and different leadership styles

Instructions

Straw Towers

1. Divide participants into groups according to leadership styles, using the results of the leadership survey completed previously. Try to keep group sizes at six to eight people.

2. Give each group twenty straws and a 25" piece of masking tape.

3. Explain that the object of the activity is to create the tallest freestanding straw tower. The masking tape can be torn into pieces and used to attach the straws together and to attach the tower to the floor but not to any other objects (such as the wall or a desk).

4. Allow ten minutes for the groups to work on their towers.

5. The tallest freestanding tower is the winner.

Create a Game

1. Divide participants into groups with at least one representative from each leadership style in each group.

2. Ask one participant from each group to collect two or three items from the materials box.

3. Instruct each group to create a game from the materials collected.

4. Allow ten minutes for the groups to create their games and game rules, and then ask each group to present its game and the rules to the larger group.

Discussion

1. After all small-group presentations, discuss the two activities using the following questions:

   - How did your group work together when all participants had similar leadership styles?

   - How did your group work together when all participants had different leadership styles?

   - Did you notice any differences?

   - What type of group was more comfortable for you—a group with similar leadership styles or a group with different leadership styles?

Optional Follow-Up

Ask participants to recall their particular leadership style and techniques that are effective when working in groups.

Grades 6–8 Adaptations

- At the beginning of this activity, review what a leadership style is and describe the different styles.

- Post a list of the leadership styles and their definitions for all participants to see.

- Depending on the ability of your group, Create a Game may not be appropriate.

BUILDING ASSETS, REDUCING RISKS
Duplicating this page is illegal. Do not duplicate without publisher's written permission.

63

Section 4: Communication

Session Title	Session Description	Materials Needed	Preparation Needed
Session 13: Nonverbals	Through an activity and discussion, participants demonstrate the power of nonverbal communication.	• Nonverbal Cues handout • Pens or pencils, one per participant • Whiteboard or Smart Board • Markers	• Print and copy the Nonverbal Cues handout, one per participant.
Session 14: Communication— Positive, Negative, or Neutral?	Through group discussion, participants recognize the impact of verbal and nonverbal communication on peers.	• Whiteboard or Smart Board • Markers • Poster board, one piece for every four to five participants • Masking tape	• Set out the poster board. • Set out markers.
Session 15: Feelings Charades	Through a team activity, participants recognize and understand how feelings affect communication.	• How Do You Feel Today? handout • Feelings Charade handout • Bowl or hat • Scissors	• Print and copy the How Do You Feel Today? handout, one per participant. • Print one copy of the Feelings Charades document.
Session 16: Effective Communication	Through activities and discussion, participants identify specific communication methods that are used to achieve a task and practice methods that will promote effective communication.	• Techniques Used to Improve Communication handout • I-Messages handout • Practicing I-Messages handout • Whiteboard or Smart Board • Markers	• Print and copy the Techniques Used to Improve Communication, I-Messages, and Practicing I-Messages handouts, one per participant.

continued

BUILDING ASSETS, REDUCING RISKS

Duplicating this page is illegal. Do not duplicate without publisher's written permission.

65

Section 4: Communication *continued*

Session Title	Session Description	Materials Needed	Preparation Needed
Session 17: Trust Dodgeball	Through this activity, participants learn that it is important to identify people in their lives they can trust and to talk with those people when making important decisions or facing difficult circumstances.	• Blindfolds, one for every two participants • Fabric or foam balls, twelve to fifteen • Small cones, twelve • Optional: large cones, twenty-four to thirty	• Reserve a large, open space for the activity, such as a basketball or tennis court, that is conducive to physical activity for twenty-four to forty participants. • Set out small cones in the activity area. • If using large cones, place them around the perimeter of the area.
Session 18: Learning to Listen	Through activities, participants recognize qualities of a good listener and also how individuals can hear the same information yet process it differently and arrive at different conclusions.	• Qualities of a Good Listener handout • Please, Just Listen document • 8½" x 11" paper, one sheet per participant • Whiteboard or Smart Board • Marker	• Print and copy the Qualities of a Good Listener, one per participant.
Session 19: Responding Skills	Through discussion, participants develop responding skills, which help show that participants understand what the speaker is saying while encouraging the speaker to share more about the problem.	• Responding Skills handout • Practice Situations for Reflective Listening handout	• Print and copy the Responding Skills and Practice Situations for Reflective Listening handouts, one per participant.
Session 20: Refusal Skills	Through a skit and discussion, participants learn how to say no in tough situations using refusal skills.	• Refusal Skills handout	• Print and copy the Refusal Skills handout, one per participant.
Session 21: What Is on Your Plate?	Through an activity and discussion, participants identify stress and stress relievers in their lives.	• Markers • Paper plates, one per participant	• Complete a sample paper plate. • Set out colored markers or crayons.

Session 13: Nonverbals

TIME NEEDED

• 20 minutes

ASSET CATEGORIES

• Social Competencies

RISK/PROTECTIVE FACTORS

• Opportunities for
  pro-social involvement

MATERIALS NEEDED

• Nonverbal Cues
  handout

• Pens or pencils,
  one per participant

• Whiteboard or
  Smart Board

• Markers

PREPARATION NEEDED

• Print and copy the
  Nonverbal Cues handout,
  one per participant.

Purpose

To demonstrate the power of nonverbal communication

Instructions

1. Ask participants to place themselves on a human continuum line by birthday, having January 1 on one end of the room and December 31 on the other. The trick is that participants must do this without talking. Hand signals are fine, but no silent mouthing of words is allowed. Give participants three minutes to complete this task. When time is up, ask each participant to state her or his birthday, starting on one end of the line. Hopefully, participants will be in order!

2. Discuss what methods participants used to communicate without talking, using these questions:

   • How did you line up sequentially by your birthday without using words?

   • What are some other ways we communicate without words?

3. Give each participant a copy of the Nonverbal Cues handout and a pen or pencil. Ask participants to write down two or three nonverbal cue examples for each category on the handout. Perhaps offer one or two examples to get people started.

4. Using the handout as a guide, lead a group discussion where participants share their examples of positive and negative nonverbal cues. Write some of the examples on the whiteboard or Smart Board.

BUILDING ASSETS, REDUCING RISKS
Duplicating this page is illegal. Do not duplicate without publisher's written permission.

67

5. Then discuss the following questions:

- When is nonverbal communication helpful? Not helpful?

- Does nonverbal communication change the way we respond in a situation?

- Using an example from the positive/negative nonverbal cue brainstorming, ask

  - What could happen if we don't pay attention to nonverbal cues?

  - What if a nonverbal cue is misread?

- What role does nonverbal communication play in our lives?

Optional Follow-Up

Periodically during the school year, remind participants of nonverbal communication and how nonverbal communication can affect all communication.

Grades 6–8 Adaptations

No adaptations are needed.

Nonverbal Cues

In the space provided, write down two or three nonverbal cue examples
for each category.

Cue	Positive Example	Negative Example
Tone of voice		
Facial expression		
Posture		
Eye contact		
Touching		
Gestures		
Spatial distance or personal space		

Session 14: Communication—
Positive, Negative, or Neutral?

- 30 minutes

- Social Competencies

- Bonding and attachment to school

- Opportunities for pro-social involvement

- Whiteboard or Smart Board

- Markers

- Poster board, one piece for every four to five participants

- Masking tape

- Set out the poster board.
- Set out markers.

Purpose

To recognize the impact of verbal and nonverbal communication on peers

Instructions

1. Ask participants to describe the different ways they communicate. Write their comments on the whiteboard or Smart Board, ensuring you are capturing words, gestures, eyes, body language, and touch. Perhaps share a few examples to get the discussion started.

2. Explain that participants are going to do an activity. In this activity, participants are going to classify the way they react to others as +, 0, and −. Write these symbols on the whiteboard or Smart Board

3. Explain the classifications:

   - Positive (+)—You like these people, you want to be around them, they make you happy or calm, they share your interests, or you think you would like them. You have a good impression of them.

   - Neutral (0)—You have no particular feelings or reactions one way or another toward these people. You may have met before, but you don't have strong reactions either positively or negatively.

   - Negative (−)—You don't enjoy being around these people. They may make you angry, sad, or just uncomfortable. Or you may not know them, but your impression is negative and you don't want to spend time with them.

4. Divide the class into small groups of four to five participants. Assign each group to one category, either +, 0,
   or –. Pass out a piece of poster board and a marker to
   each group. Ask the shortest person in each group to be
   the recorder—the person writing the group's ideas on
   the poster board.

5. Ask the person whose birthday is closest to today (in either
   direction) to be the reporter, who will share the group's
   work with the whole class. Have the recorders write their
   group sign at the top of their poster board (either +, 0, or –).

6. Write a series of scenarios on the whiteboard or Smart
   Board. Write one scenario down at a time. After each
   scenario, have the groups discuss how they would respond
   to the person in that situation given their assigned
   category (+, 0, or –). Challenge groups to consider all
   forms of communication (such as words, actions, or facial
   expressions). If needed, work through the first scenario
   together so participants understand the exercise.

7. Allow approximately three to five minutes for the groups
   to discuss each scenario and for the recorder to write the
   group's ideas on the poster board. Tell the recorder to
   leave enough room to record ideas for six scenarios.

   Here are the scenarios:

   • You see this person walking toward you in the school
     hallway. You are alone.

   • You see this person walking toward you in the school
     hallway and you are with a group of friends.

   • This person sits down next to you in class.

   • This person asks to borrow a pencil.

   • This person is assigned to work with you on a class
     assignment.

   • This person invites you to a party.

NOTES

8. After all of the scenarios have been discussed and answers have been recorded, have each group tape its poster board on the wall. Pick two or three scenarios and ask the group reporters to share what their teams wrote.

9. After each reporter has shared, discuss these questions:

   • Why respond this way?

   • How might that response feel to the person?

10. Now put all the + responses together. Ask the group how it would feel to go through your day encountering these reactions all day long. Repeat this same process for the negative responses. Discuss whether this effect is intentional or necessary.

▶ Facilitator note: This prompt helps to illustrate the cumulative impact of the verbals and nonverbals on a student.

11. Do the same process for the neutral responses last. Have participants consider this response in more depth. Who are the people that we typically respond to in a neutral manner? These people are often almost invisible. Maybe they just moved here. Maybe they are shy. You don't think you are hurting them, but how would it feel to encounter this reaction all day long?

12. Based on what the group learned today, talk about how participants could treat people differently in real life.

Optional Follow-Up

Revisit this topic as school climate issues occur during the school year.

Grades 6–8 Adaptations

Consider role playing these response scenarios with another participant to encourage ideas and participation. It might be easier to role play one response per group to get the activity started. If participants still have trouble, role play all possible responses to each scenario while participants remain in a large group.

The author wishes to thank Carley Kregness for this I-Time session. Carley has been a Building Assets, Reducing Risks *facilitator for over a decade.*

NOTES

BUILDING ASSETS, REDUCING RISKS
Duplicating this page is illegal. Do not duplicate without publisher's written permission.

73

Session 15: Feelings Charades

TIME NEEDED

• 30 minutes

ASSET CATEGORIES

• Social Competencies
• Support

RISK/PROTECTIVE FACTORS

• Opportunities for
pro-social involvement

MATERIALS NEEDED

• How Do You Feel
Today? handout

• Feelings Charade
handout

• Scissors

• Hat or bowl

PREPARATION NEEDED

• Print and copy the
How Do You Feel
Today? handout,
one per participant.

• Print the Feelings
Charade document and
cut apart the slips with
one feeling per slip.

Place all the slips into
a hat or bowl.

Purpose

To recognize and understand how feelings
affect communication

Instructions

1. Give each student a copy of the How Do You Feel Today?
   handout. Students can use this handout for reference
   during the game, if needed.

2. Divide participants into teams of five or six.
   Inform participants that they will be playing a
   type of charades game.

3. Have each team choose a representative to receive a
   Feelings Charade slip (draw a feeling slip from the hat).

4. The representative silently reads the feeling listed on the
   slip of paper and then returns to his or her group but does
   not tell anyone the feeling.

5. When all representatives have returned to their teams,
   give a signal for the representatives to begin acting out
   the feelings on their slips. The first team to guess the
   feeling correctly stands up. Track the points for each team
   (one point for each correct answer that is stated first).

6. Repeat this process, rotating representatives from each
   team to ensure that all participants have a turn to act out
   a feeling.

7. Lead a group discussion using the following questions:

   • Is it difficult to identify some feelings?
     Why is it difficult?

   • How do feelings affect our behavior?

BUILDING ASSETS, REDUCING RISKS
Duplicating this page is illegal. Do not duplicate without publisher's written permission.

74

• Do we sometimes show one feeling but actually have another feeling? For example, have you ever been angry but didn't show your anger? Or happy but did not show your happiness? Why do we do this sometimes?

• Remember our class on nonverbal communication? How might nonverbal cues affect you when you show one feeling but feel a different one?

• How do our feelings affect our communication?

Optional Follow-Up

Periodically throughout the year, encourage participants to remember how both verbal communication and nonverbal cues can affect communication.

Grades 6–8 Adaptations

• Use only the bolded words on the Feelings Charade handout.

• Simplify the questions asked in step 7:

  – Is it hard to know what someone is feeling? Why?

  – Do you look different when you're angry versus when you're happy?

  – Do we sometimes hide what we feel by showing a different face? For example, have you ever been angry but didn't show your anger? Or happy but did not show your happiness? Why does this happen?

  – How do our feelings affect how we talk to one another?

  – Have you ever thought someone was happy when they weren't? Why did you think they were happy?

NOTES

How Do You Feel Today?

 AGGRESSIVE   AGONIZED   ANXIOUS   APOLOGETIC   ARROGANT   BASHFUL   BLISSFUL

 BORED   CAUTIOUS   COLD   CONCENTRATING   CONFIDENT   CURIOUS   DEMURE

 DETERMINED   DISAPPOINTED   DISAPPROVING   DISBELIEVING   DISGUSTED   DISTASTEFUL   FRUSTRATED

 ECSTATIC   ENRAGED   ENVIOUS   EXASPERATED   EXHAUSTED   FRIGHTENED   HURT

 GRIEVING   GUILTY   HAPPY   HORRIFIED   INTERESTED   JEALOUS   JOYFUL

 HYSTERICAL   INDIFFERENT   LOVESTRUCK   INNOCENT   MISCHIEVOUS   MISERABLE   NEGATIVE

 OBSTINATE   LONELY   PAINED   MEDITATIVE   PERPLEXED   PRUDISH   PUZZLED

 REGRETFUL   OPTIMISTIC   SAD   PARANOID   SHOCKED   UNDECIDED   SMUG

 SURPRISED   RELIEVED   SUSPICIOUS   SATISFIED   THOUGHTFUL   SYMPATHETIC   WITHDRAWN

Feelings Charade

Copy this page and cut it into slips with one feeling per slip.
Place the slips in a hat or bowl.

AGGRESSIVE	EXHAUSTED	MISERABLE
ANXIOUS	*FRIGHTENED*	OPTIMISTIC
ARROGANT	FRUSTRATED	PARANOID
BASHFUL	*GUILTY*	PUZZLED
BORED	*HAPPY*	RELIEVED
CONFIDENT	HURT	*SAD*
CURIOUS	INNOCENT	SHOCKED
DISAPPOINTED	JEALOUS	*SURPRISED*
DISGUSTED	JOYFUL	SYMPATHETIC
EXCITED	LONELY	WITHDRAWN

Session 16: Effective Communication

TIME NEEDED

• 1 hour

ASSET CATEGORIES

• Social Competencies
• Support

RISK/PROTECTIVE FACTORS

• Opportunities for
  pro-social involvement

MATERIALS NEEDED

• Techniques Used
  to Improve
  Communication
  handout

• I-Messages handout

• Practicing
  I-Messages handout

• Whiteboard or
  Smart Board

• Markers

PREPARATION NEEDED

• Print and copy the
  three handouts, one copy
  per participant.

Purpose

• To identify specific communication methods used to
  achieve a task

• To practice methods that will promote effective
  communication

Instructions

Knots

1. Line up participants from shortest to tallest.

2. Divide into groups of six to eight participants who are
   of similar height.

3. Ask each group to stand in a circle.

4. Instruct participants to reach across the circle with their
   right hand and hold the right hand of the person across
   from them and, with their left hand, reach across the
   circle and take the left hand of a different person. Make
   sure everyone is holding the hands of two different people.
   Explain that the object of the activity is for participants
   to untangle themselves from the knot without letting go
   of any hands. (The group will be tangled just by the
   manner in which members are holding hands.) Allow five
   to ten minutes for the groups to complete the task.

▶ Facilitator note: Not all groups will be able to untangle their group knot.

5. After they are done untangling their knots, discuss the
   activity using the following questions:

   • What helped your group untangle your knot?

   • Did your group have a leader?

   • If there was a leader, how did he or she communicate
     to other group members?

• Was untangling your knot accomplished by trial and error?

• If you didn't untangle your knot, why were you unable to do so?

• Were there techniques of communication that were helpful? Unhelpful?

6. Lead a large group discussion exploring techniques that improve communication. Ask participants to brainstorm techniques that improve communication. List all of their ideas on the whiteboard or Smart Board.

7. Give each participant a copy of the Techniques Used to Improve Communication handout. Compare the brainstormed list generated by participants to the handout, looking for similarities and differences. Then ask participants:

• Are these concepts understandable? Usable?

• How might these techniques help communication?

8. Explain that one effective communication technique is using I-messages, which will be explored in the next activity.

I-Messages

1. Explain that expressing feelings in I-messages increases effective communication.

2. Give each participant a copy of the I-Messages handout and review it with the class.

3. Divide participants into pairs.

4. Give each participant a copy of the Practicing I-Messages handout. Have each pair work together to develop I-messages for the first two examples on the handout. Then have each participant choose a personal example and write an I-message for that example.

BUILDING ASSETS, REDUCING RISKS
Duplicating this page is illegal. Do not duplicate without publisher's written permission.

79

5. Have pairs take turns reading their I-messages from their personal example to their partner.

6. Facilitate a discussion with the whole group about giving and receiving I-messages, using the following questions:

    • What are your thoughts about using I-messages?

    • What challenges did you experience using an I-message?

    • Were you able to state your feelings?

    • Describe your feelings as you heard the I-message.

    • What suggestions or feedback do you have for the person who gave you the I-message?

Grades 6–8 Adaptations

    • Simplify the questions for step 5 of the Knots activity:

        – What helped your group untangle the knot?

        – Did your group have a leader?

        – If there was a leader, how did he or she communicate to other group members?

        – Did you make any mistakes?

        – Did you learn from them?

        – If you did not untangle your group, what made it difficult?

    • Skip the discussion in step 6 of the I-Messages activity.

Techniques Used to Improve Communication

Following are some techniques you can try to improve your communication with others.

- Look at (make eye contact with) the person to whom you are speaking.

- Speak clearly.

- Calmly say what you are *feeling*. (Don't whine or yell.)

- After talking, *listen*—don't just hear.

Remember these communication tips:

- Be aware of how much distance is between you and the person you are talking to—be situated close enough so you can talk and hear each other easily. (Avoid communicating across a room.)

- Be direct—ask for what you want.

- Listen more than you speak.

- Listen to the other person speaking without interrupting.

- Avoid following the person's statement with a lecture.

1 of 1

I-Messages

I-messages are statements used to effectively communicate your feelings without blaming the other person. They express how you feel and why you feel as you do.

For example:

"I feel angry when you borrow my clothes without asking."

I-messages are the opposite of "you" messages. "You" messages are negative approaches to resolving conflicts and usually only cause things to get worse.

For example:

"You are stupid and inconsiderate! Don't you know to ask someone before you borrow his or her things?"

I-messages should be clear, concise, honest, and an accurate expression of how you feel and why.

Example scenario:

Marcus's sister promised to do Marcus's chores while he spent the night at the neighbors' house. When Marcus gets home, he finds out that his dog has not been fed.

Example of an I-message that Marcus could use with his sister:

"I feel angry when the dog isn't fed because you promised to do my chores."

Practicing I-Messages

Practice writing I-messages for the scenarios below.

1. Ashley and Maria agree to meet at the movie theater at 1:00 p.m. Ashley shows up forty minutes late and doesn't even offer an apology.

    What I-message could Maria use?

    I feel _____ when _____ because_____.

2. You loaned your science book to Mark. Mark promised to return the book to you today (which is Wednesday), and Mark just told you he can't find the book. There is a science test on Friday.

    What I-message could you say to Mark?

    I feel _____ when _____ because_____.

3. Recall an event where you needed to express your feelings. For example, your brother used your ball for practice without asking, or your friend went to the mall without telling you there was a change in plans.

    Describe your situation:

    _____

    _____

    _____

    _____

    _____

    What I-message could you use in this situation?

    I feel _____ when _____ because_____.

Session 17: Trust Dodgeball

TIME NEEDED

- At least 45 minutes

ASSET CATEGORIES

- Social Competencies

RISK PROTECTIVE FACTOR

- Pro-social involvement

MATERIALS NEEDED

- Blindfolds, one for every two participants

- Very soft fabric or foam balls, like those made by Nerf, twelve to fifteen (Ask your physical education department to loan you squishy dodgeballs. Rubber balls or any stiff ball should not be used.)

- Twelve small cones, to be used as obstacles in the space

- Optional: Twenty-four to thirty larger cones (to mark the space perimeter if a permanently lined space is not available)

PREPARATION NEEDED

- Set up the cones in the outdoor area.

SPACE NEEDED

A space that is conducive to physical activity; one half of a basketball court or tennis court is ideal for a class of twenty-four to forty participants (It is important that half of the class can position themselves around the outside of the space on all sides.)

Purpose

- To help participants understand the importance of identifying people in their lives they can trust

- To help participants understand the importance of communicating with those people when making important decisions or facing difficult circumstances

Instructions

1. Explain that in order to be successful in this game, participants must actively depend on one other participant and communicate with that person.

2. Pair participants (use one group of three if numbers are odd and then allow enough time to play at least three rounds). Then share the following:

   - For today's activity, the person you are paired with represents the people in your life whom you can trust and who have your best interests in mind.

   - You will need to communicate with them clearly and trust only them.

   - There will be a lot of commotion and distractions in this activity, so make sure you commit to listening only to your partner.

- Just like in this game, life will present you with hard decisions and difficult situations. We all need people we can turn to for advice and help, and your partner is representing that type of person in the activity today.

3. Explain the game and the rules:

- We will play at least two rounds of a game called Trust Dodgeball. If time allows, we will play additional rounds.

- In this game, one person from each pair will be blindfolded and moved to the inside of the game area. The blindfolded partner will try to locate balls, stay inside the game area (describe the playing space), avoid obstacles (cones), avoid being hit by balls that are tossed, and attempt to hit other blindfolded participants.

- The people who are not blindfolded will be the eyes for their blindfolded partner. They must stay on the outside of the playing space but are free to move around the perimeter. They may give directions to their partner. They may also retrieve balls that leave the space and hand them to their partner, but they are not allowed to throw balls.

- Blindfolded players cannot run or throw balls overhand. Overhand throws will eliminate you from the round since they can lead to hands hitting faces. Also, speed on the ball is not important since the people you're trying to hit can't see.

- Blindfolded players are out of the game if they break a rule or if they step on a perimeter line, touch a cone set up as an obstacle, or are hit by a ball. A ball that bounces before it hits a person does not count.

- The game will be played until only one blindfolded participant remains.

BUILDING ASSETS, REDUCING RISKS
Duplicating this page is illegal. Do not duplicate without publisher's written permission.

85

4. Instruct pairs to decide which person is going to be blindfolded first and pass out a blindfold to each pair. Inspect whether the blindfold is positioned correctly. If it is, then the sighted participants can move their partners to the location of their choice in the playing space and then remove themselves from the inside of the playing area.

5. Keep the balls in a bag until all the sighted players are outside of the playing area and the blindfolded participants are ready. Then distribute the balls randomly with a quick dump of the bag and yell "Go!" During the first round, the facilitator can move around and play referee and announce when participants are out. Also announce when there are only three players left and when only two remain.

6. Variations on the facilitator role: In the second and following rounds, the facilitator could represent added obstacles in life:

- Move cones in position to make it more difficult for some participants. You could even surround a participant with three or four cones.

- Since participants are only supposed to listen and trust their partners, ask blindfolded players to take your hand so you can lead them to a ball, but then actually lead them out of the space. (Be sure to debrief with the participants why this was done in the context of the simulation so they don't exit the game feeling cheated.)

- Hand balls to blindfolded players or place balls right at their feet to speed up a slow round.

7. Debriefing time: Have participants take off the blindfolds and have the whole group sit down. Ask them three key questions for discussion:

   - What things did I share at the beginning about the purpose of this game?

   - What went well for you and your partner, and what was difficult?

   - What are some real-life situations that could be made better by the help of someone we can trust and listen to?

8. End with one personal question that participants can elect to share or just keep to themselves:

   - If you were suddenly faced with a very difficult decision or a very troubling situation, who are the people you feel you can trust and turn to for help?

   - You could also ask them to think of three specific people: one peer, one adult family member, and one adult outside their family. This step could also be used as a "next day" journaling activity.

9. Cleanup: Have participants assist with retrieving balls and cones and untying knots in blindfolds in preparation for the next class.

Optional Follow-Up

Throughout the school year, revisit the list of people the participants know they can trust.

Grades 6–8 Adaptations

No adaptations are needed.

BUILDING ASSETS, REDUCING RISKS
Duplicating this page is illegal. Do not duplicate without publisher's written permission.

87

Session 18: Learning to Listen

TIME NEEDED

- 30 minutes

ASSET CATEGORIES

- Social Competencies
- Support

RISK/PROTECTIVE FACTORS

- Opportunities for pro-social involvement

MATERIALS NEEDED

- Qualities of a Good Listener handout
- Optional: Please, Just Listen handout
- 8½" x 11" paper, one sheet per participant
- Whiteboard or Smart Board
- Marker

PREPARATION NEEDED

- Print and copy the Qualities of a Good Listener handout, one per participant.
- Optional: Print and copy the Please, Just Listen handout, one per participant.

Purpose

- To recognize qualities of a good listener
- To recognize how individuals can hear the same information yet process it differently and arrive at different conclusions

Instructions

1. Give each participant a piece of paper.

2. Read the following Paper Tear Directions aloud, asking participants to follow the directions without talking or asking questions. Only read these directions. Don't answer participants' questions or otherwise try to clarify the directions.

——————— Paper Tear Directions ———————

- Fold your paper in half like a hot dog bun.
- Now close your eyes.
- Tear off the left-hand corner, keeping your eyes closed.
- Also keeping your eyes closed, fold the paper into a square.
- Now tear off the bottom left-hand corner.
- Fold the paper one more time, and tear off the left-hand corner.
- Open your eyes and unfold the paper.

3. Ask all participants to hold their papers over their heads, and compare the results. All the papers will likely look very different.

4. After the Paper Tear exercise is done, ask the following questions:

   • Are there any papers that are similar?

   • Are there more paper tears that are different than the same?

   • How can everyone hear the same thing yet our papers look so different?

5. Ask participants to brainstorm qualities of a good listener, and list their ideas on the whiteboard or Smart Board.

6. Distribute the Qualities of a Good Listener handout and review it with the class. Compare the brainstormed list on the whiteboard or Smart Board with the handout, and discuss the similarities as well as the differences. Compliment participants on listing the qualities of good listeners, no matter how many similarities are actually a match.

7. Read "Please, Just Listen" to all participants (page 92). A copy of this poem is included as an optional handout if you wish to use it.

8. Discuss the following questions:

   • What do you hear the author trying to say?

   • What is he or she expecting?

   • Think about this quote from the reading, "When I ask you to listen to me and you feel you have to do something to solve my problem, you have failed me." How is this a failure?

   • What does the author mean when he or she says, "When you do something for me that I can and need to do for myself, you may contribute to my fear and inadequacy"?

BUILDING ASSETS, REDUCING RISKS
Duplicating this page is illegal. Do not duplicate without publisher's written permission.

89

Optional Follow-Up

Throughout the year, remind participants how perception affects communication.

Grades 6–8 Adaptations

No adaptations are needed.

Qualities of a Good Listener

Here are some qualities of a **GOOD LISTENER:**

- does not need to solve the problem

- does not need to tell the other person what to do

- does not see things as either black or white

- is empathetic and tries to understand things from the other person's perspective

- can pick up on others' feelings

- is authentic—comes across as genuine and not phony

- is skilled at seeking out alternatives

- is responsible

- respects himself or herself and the person who is speaking

- has the ability to be specific

- is honest

- is comfortable with appropriate self-disclosure (can share about personal experience)

- looks the other person in the eyes while listening

- is comfortable with confrontation; can tell it like it is with gentleness

- doesn't interrupt; lets the other person speak

- does not tell others about the conversation; respects the other person's privacy

Please, Just Listen

When I ask you to listen to me and you start giving advice,
you have not done what I asked.

When I ask you to listen to me and you begin to tell me why I shouldn't feel that way,
you are trampling on my feelings.

When I ask you to listen to me and you feel you have to do something to solve my problem,
you have failed me, strange as that may seem.

Listen! All I asked was that you listen, not talk or do . . . just hear.

Advice is cheap: seventy-five cents will get you both Dear Abby and Billy Graham in the
same newspaper.

And I can do for myself. I am not helpless.
Maybe discouraged and faltering, but not helpless.

When you do something for me that I can and need to do for myself,
you contribute to my fear and inadequacy.

But when you accept as a simple fact that I do feel,
no matter how irrational, then I can quit trying to convince you and get about the
business of understanding what's behind this irrational feeling.

And when that's clear, the answers are obvious and I don't need advice.
Irrational feelings make sense when we understand what's behind them.

So please just listen and just hear me.
And if you want to talk, wait a minute for your turn,
and I'll listen to you.

This poem (in various versions) has been attributed to multiple sources. Most frequently, the author is either cited as "Anonymous" (first appearing in the 1977 book *Therapeutic Approaches to the Care of the Mentally Ill,* by David S. and Sharon O. Bailey-Dreyer) or as "Ray Houghton, M.D., of Berkeley, Calif." (first appearing in *Teen Times,* the official publication of the Future Homemakers of America, now called Family, Career, and Community Leaders of America).

 **Section 4:
Communication**

Session 19: Responding Skills

- 30 minutes

- Social Competencies

- Opportunities for
pro-social involvement

- Responding Skills
handout

- Practice Situations
for Reflective
Listening handout

- Print and copy the
two handouts, one copy
per participant.

Purpose

To develop responding skills; responding skills help show the speaker we understand what he or she is saying while encouraging the speaker to continue sharing

Instructions

1. Distribute the Responding Skills handout. Using the handout, explain what responding skills are and the six different responding skills (paraphrasing, reflecting, clarifying, open-ended questions, closed-ended questions, and why questions) to the large group.

2. Divide participants into groups of three.

3. Distribute the Practice Situations for Reflective Listening handout. Ask participants to use one of the scenarios on the handout or have them develop their own situations to practice using responding skills. One person in each group will present the problem, one person will practice the responding skill (such as paraphrasing), and one person will give feedback on how well the responding skill is being used. Repeat with two more scenarios, rotate roles.

4. After each group has completed three scenarios, lead a large group discussion using the following questions:

   - Describe your feelings while you were practicing responding skills (such as paraphrasing, reflecting, or clarifying). What challenges did you face?

   - Describe your feelings when you received feedback. (Did you feel sad or excited?) How did the listener's feedback affect your conversation?

   - Did anyone use or receive why questions? How did why questions help or hinder your communication?

Duplicating this page is illegal. Do not duplicate without publisher's written permission.

93

Optional Follow-Up

Assist participants with responding skills throughout
the year.

Grades 6–8 Adaptations

This exercise might be a stretch for younger participants,
so ensure that participants understand the exercise by giving
multiple examples of the different kinds of responses either
through a discussion or role plays. If needed, demonstrate
the skills in front of the whole group.

Responding Skills

Responding is what we say after we have listened. Helpful responding has two goals:

1. To show the speaker we understand her or him

2. To encourage the speaker to continue talking about her or his problem

Responding skills include

Paraphrasing: Saying in different words what someone has said.

For example:

- "I wish I didn't come to baseball practice. Everyone puts me down."

    Paraphrase: "People on the team insult you, so you'd rather stay home."

Reflecting: Mirroring or reflecting back the other person's feelings.

This skill has three parts:

1. Stating what you think the person feels. "It sounds like you feel sad."

2. Stating what you think caused the feeling. "It seems that you feel sad because you lost the race."

3. Checking with the person to make sure your reflection was accurate. "Am I right?" or just pause and let the person's body language tell you whether you were right.

Reflecting usually follows this format: "You feel . . . because . . . Is that it?"

Paraphrasing and reflecting show others that we understand them and encourage them to continue talking.

Clarifying: When you aren't sure you understand what the person is saying, ask clarifying questions.

For example:

- "Do I understand you? Are you saying . . . ?"
- "I think I got lost. Could you go over it again?"

1 of 2

Open-ended Questions: These are the most helpful type of questions; they require more than a one-word or a yes/no answer.

For example:

- "What did you do when that happened?"
- "How does that make things different?"

Closed-ended Questions: These do not encourage the speaker to continue talking; they only require a one-word or a yes/no answer.

For example:

- "How old were you when you moved?"
- "Did that make you angry?"

Why Questions: These questions focus on reasons and can make the person feel defensive. Balance asking questions with other responses. Asking too many questions can make the person feel as though he or she is being investigated rather than helped.

BUILDING ASSETS, REDUCING RISKS

Practice Situations
for Reflective Listening

Use one of the scenarios to practice using responding skills.

Situation 1: "I'd like to hang out with Kendra, but my mom says she doesn't like her because she is a bad influence."

Situation 2: "I'm going to Juan's party tonight. I think there is going to be drinking. I hope I'm not the only one who doesn't want to drink."

Situation 3: "I was asked to the Homecoming Dance but my dad won't let me go. He says ninth graders are too young to go to dances."

Situation 4: "Ms. Green is a horrible teacher. She doesn't know how to explain things, and I'm not ready for the test tomorrow."

Situation 5: "My parents are always on my back. They always want to know where I am, what I'm doing, and who I'm with. They never leave me alone."

Situation 6: "I hate gym class! People never pick me to be on their team."

Situation 7: "Coach Chang hates me. I should have made the team. I was better than DeShawn and he made it."

Situation 8: "I saw Alec take a watch from the store and not pay for it. I don't know what to do."

Situation 9: "My mother told our neighbors I would babysit for them on Friday night, but I wanted to go to the game. My mom says I owe it to our neighbors since they are always helping me out."

Situation 10: "I hate it here—nobody talks to me. I wish I was back at my old school— at least I had fun there."

1 of 1

Session 20: Refusal Skills

TIME NEEDED

• 30 minutes or more, depending on the number of small groups

ASSET CATEGORIES

• Social Competencies

RISK/PROTECTIVE FACTORS

• Opportunities for pro-social involvement

MATERIALS NEEDED

• Refusal Skills handout

PREPARATION NEEDED

• Print and copy the Refusal Skills handout, one per participant.

Purpose

To learn how to say no in tough situations using refusal skills

Instructions

1. Distribute and discuss the Refusal Skills handout as a large group.

2. Divide the class into groups of five to seven participants.

3. Ask each group to think of a high-risk activity (such as cheating on a test, skipping class, using alcohol or other drugs). Then instruct each group to develop a skit that demonstrates how the five-step refusal skills model described in the handout can be used when faced with the high-risk activity the group has identified. Give the groups about ten minutes to plan and practice their skits.

4. Have each small group introduce its high-risk activity and then present its skit to the larger group.

5. Debrief after each skit using the following questions:

Questions for the person who was refusing the activity in the skit:

   • What were your thoughts about the person who was pushing you to do the high-risk activity?

   • How did you feel about your response?

   • After thinking about your situation, would you have done anything differently?

Questions for the person who was trying to push the activity in the skit:

- What were your thoughts about the person you were trying to convince to do a risky behavior?

- How did you feel about his or her response?

- Would you have done anything differently?

Questions for the general group:

- What are your thoughts about the skit? How did it go? (Caution: Don't allow participants to make fun of others' acting.)

- Could you see the five steps being used?

- Did they work?

- Any suggestions or additional ideas to help the person refuse?

6. Compliment the groups for their creativity and willingness to use refusal skills. Also thank group members for their suggestions!

Optional Follow-Up

Assist participants with refusal skills throughout the year.

Grades 6–8 Adaptations

No adaptations are needed.

BUILDING ASSETS, REDUCING RISKS

Duplicating this page is illegal. Do not duplicate without publisher's written permission.

99

Refusal Skills

How to Say No When It Is Difficult

People who know how to use refusal skills are more likely to make positive choices and avoid or get out of high-risk situations. Setting limits and feeling confident in saying no to outside pressures increases a person's self-confidence. Learning to stop and consider the consequences before responding to a request helps individuals become more accomplished at refusing to participate in things that could harm themselves or others.

Four goals of using refusal skills:

1. To stay in control
2. To keep your friends
3. To have fun
4. To stay out of trouble

The five-step refusal skills model:

1. Ask questions.
2. Think about your decision (name the trouble).
3. State the consequences.
4. Sell the alternative.
5. Move and leave the door open.

Here is an example of how to say no in a tough situation using the five-step refusal skills model.

Your friend wants you to use drugs:

1. **Ask questions:** "What if we get caught?"

2. **Think about your decision:** "My parents would ground me and I might lose eligibility for the basketball season."

3. **State the consequences:** "I would be grounded and lose eligibility for the basketball season."

4. **Sell the alternative:** "How about going to a movie or hanging out at the gym?"

5. **Move and leave the door open:** If your friend still wants to use drugs, say, "I have to go, but I'll see you later."

1 of 1

Session 21: What Is on Your Plate?

TIME NEEDED

• 30 minutes

ASSET CATEGORIES

• Positive Identity

RISK/PROTECTIVE FACTORS

• Opportunities for pro-social involvement

MATERIALS NEEDED

• Markers

• Paper plates, one per participant

• Colored markers or crayons

PREPARATION NEEDED

• Complete a sample paper plate for this exercise. The facilitator should use her or his own life as the example.

• Set out colored markers or crayons.

Purpose

• To identify stress

• To identify stress relievers

Instructions

1. Hand out a paper plate to each participant.

2. Instruct participants to divide their plates into four sections and label the sections: Activities, Interests, Responsibilities, and Miscellaneous.

3. In each corresponding section of the plate, tell participants to write what is going on in this area of their lives right now. Before participants start, show the example that you completed. Allow five to ten minutes for this activity.

4. After the paper plates are completed, ask the participants to think about the things on their plates that

   • they enjoy the most

   • take the most time

   • they would like to spend more time doing

   • drain most of their energy

   • energize them the most

   • they can do without

5. Have the participants turn to a partner and take turns sharing their answers to the questions above.

6. Facilitate a whole group discussion on what participants learned about themselves and their partners. Model the discussion by sharing your answers first.

7. Ask participants if they could make different choices about how they spend their time, what they would change. Allow several people to respond.

BUILDING ASSETS, REDUCING RISKS

Duplicating this page is illegal. Do not duplicate without publisher's written permission.

101

Optional Follow-Up

Prior to testing periods or other high-stress times in school, ask participants to recall what activities help them relieve stress. Encourage participants to devote time to stress-relieving activities.

Grades 6–8 Adaptations

No adaptations are needed.

The author would like to acknowledge Kelly Brown for this I-Time activity. She has been a Building Assets, Reducing Risks *facilitator for over a decade.*

Section 5: Assets Activities

Session Title	Session Description	Materials Needed	Preparation Needed
Session 22: What Are Your Assets?	Through filling out handouts and a discussion, participants analyze their own assets and compare their responses to those of others.	• Asset Checklist handout • Developmental Assets among American Youth handout • Assets by Grade and Gender handout • Pens or pencils, one per participant	• Print and copy the three handouts, one per participant.
Session 23: Support Web	Through an activity, participants identify sources of support in their lives.	• Beach ball • Yarn, enough to make a web	• Clear an area in your room so participants can sit in a circle.
Session 24: Golden Nuggets	Through an activity, participants identify their own personal value and worth, and the importance of building their Developmental Assets.	• Rocks of different sizes, one per participant	• None needed.

BUILDING ASSETS, REDUCING RISKS
Duplicating this page is illegal. Do not duplicate without publisher's written permission.

103

Assets Activities

Session 22: What Are Your Assets?

TIME NEEDED

- 1 hour

ASSET CATEGORIES

- Positive Identity

RISK/PROTECTIVE FACTORS

- Opportunities for pro-social improvement

MATERIALS NEEDED

- Asset Checklist handout
- Developmental Assets among American Youth handout
- Assets by Grade and Gender handout
- Pens or pencils, one per participant

PREPARATION NEEDED

- Print and copy the three handouts, one copy per participant.

Purpose

To help participants analyze their own assets and compare their responses to those of thousands of students surveyed by the Search Institute, creators of the Developmental Assets theory

Instructions

1. Explain what assets are. (For example: Assets are those positive things in a person's life that help the person do well.) Distribute the Asset Checklist handout and a pen or pencil to each participant. Assure participants that no one else will look at their answers on this handout, so they can be honest with themselves. They will be asked to share only what they want to share. Have participants fill out the handout.

2. Distribute the Developmental Assets among American Youth and the Assets by Grade and Gender handouts. Encourage participants to compare their answers to the nationwide results provided on these handouts.

3. Discuss assets using the following discussion points and questions:

   - Most young people experience many of these assets. Here are the top four assets that young people report having in their lives:

     – Asset 40—feeling optimistic about their personal futures (75 percent)

     – Asset 1—having a family life that provides high levels of love and support (72 percent)

     – Asset 21—feeling motivated to do well in school (71 percent)

     – Asset 28—acting on convictions and standing up for beliefs (71 percent)

- How do your assets compare with those of other young people?

- In what ways are your assets similar to or different from youth surveyed by Search Institute, a national organization that promotes assets among young people?

- Why do you think your answers are similar or different?

- Most young people are also missing certain other assets. Here are the four assets that most young people do not have in their lives:

  - Asset 17—spending three or more hours per week in sessions or practice in music, theater, or other arts (20 percent)

  - Asset 25—reading for pleasure three or more hours per week (23 percent)

  - Asset 7—perceiving that adults in the community value youth (25 percent)

  - Asset 14—having parents(s) and other adults who model positive, responsible behavior (28 percent)

- How many of these assets do you have in your life?

- How important do you think these assets are? Why?

- Why do you think researchers have said assets are important in growing up healthy?

4. Continue the discussion of assets with the following information:

- Assets are separated into internal assets and external assets. Assets 1–20 are considered external assets, meaning they are things outside of yourself that can help you grow up healthy. These include support, empowerment, boundaries and expectations, and constructive use of time. Assets 21–40 are considered internal assets, meaning they are things you can cultivate within yourself that help you grow up healthy. These include commitment to learning, positive values, social competencies, and positive identity.

    – Do you have more internal assets or external assets?

    – Why do you think that is?

- The data from Search Institute indicates that the average number of assets youth report is about twenty. Look at how many assets you checked True.

    – How similar or different are you to other youth nationally?

- Also compare yourself to others in your grade and others of your gender.

    – Why do you think older youth have fewer assets compared with younger youth?

    – Why do you think females have more assets than males?

    – Where do you experience these assets in your own life?

    – Is it mostly at home, at school, or in other places?

    – When have you found one or more of these assets to be really important in helping you through a tough time or with a hard decision?

5. Divide the class into smaller groups of four to five participants. Encourage them to discuss their asset levels in the small group.

6. Assign an asset to each small group, asking them to brainstorm strategies to promote that asset. Here are some possible choices: assets 5, 8, 15, 34, and 36.

7. Ask each small group to present their ideas to the larger group.

Optional Follow-Up

Use the asset framework when discussing school and community issues.

Grades 6–8 Adaptations

- Simplify the definition of the word *asset*, for example:

    - An asset is also known as a strength. The more assets you have, the less likely it is that you will take part in risky behaviors.

Reprinted with permission from Building Assets Together *by Jolene L. Roehlkepartain. Copyright © 1997 by Search Institute®, Minneapolis, MN; 800-888-7828; www.search -institute.org. Data has been revised using the 2010 data set.*

BUILDING ASSETS, REDUCING RISKS

Duplicating this page is illegal. Do not duplicate without publisher's written permission.

107

Asset Checklist

Many young people experience too few of the Developmental Assets. Check whether each statement is true or false for you to get an idea of areas where you experience a lot of assets and areas where you could use more assets.

External Assets

Support

1.	I receive lots of love and support from my family.	T	F
2.	My parent(s) and I communicate positively, and I am willing to go to my parent(s) for advice and counsel.	T	F
3.	I receive support from three or more nonparent adults.	T	F
4.	I experience caring neighbors.	T	F
5.	My school provides a caring, encouraging environment.	T	F
6.	My parent(s) are actively involved in helping me succeed in school.	T	F

Empowerment

7.	I believe that adults in the community value youth.	T	F
8.	I believe that young people are given useful roles in the community.	T	F
9.	I serve in my community for one hour or more per week.	T	F
10.	I feel safe at home, at school, and in the neighborhood.	T	F

Boundaries and Expectations

11.	My family has clear rules and consequences, and monitors my whereabouts.	T	F
12.	My school provides clear rules and consequences.	T	F
13.	My neighbors take responsibility for monitoring young people's behavior.	T	F
14.	Parent(s) and other adults model positive, responsible behavior.	T	F

1 of 3

15. My best friends model responsible behavior.	T	F
16. Both my parent(s) and my teachers encourage me to do well.	T	F

Constructive Use of Time

17. I spend three hours or more per week in sessions or practice in music, theater, or other arts.	T	F
18. I spend three hours or more per week in sports, clubs, and organizations at school and/or in the community.	T	F
19. I spend one or more hours per week in activities in a religious institution.	T	F
20. I go with friends "with nothing special to do" two or fewer nights per week.	T	F

Internal Assets

Commitment to Learning

21. I am motivated to do well in school.	T	F
22. I am actively engaged in learning.	T	F
23. I do at least one hour of homework every school day.	T	F
24. I care about my school.	T	F
25. I read for pleasure three or more hours per week.	T	F

Positive Values

26. I place a high value on helping other people.	T	F
27. I place a high value on promoting equality and reducing hunger and poverty.	T	F
28. I act on my convictions and stand up for my beliefs.	T	F
29. I tell the truth even when it is not easy.	T	F
30. I accept and take personal responsibility.	T	F
31. I believe it is important not to be sexually active or to use alcohol or other drugs.	T	F

2 of 3

Social Competencies

32. I know how to plan ahead and make choices.	T	F
33. I have empathy, sensitivity, and friendship skills.	T	F
34. I have knowledge of and comfort with people of different cultural/racial/ethnic backgrounds.	T	F
35. I can resist negative peer pressure and dangerous situations.	T	F
36. I seek to resolve conflict nonviolently.	T	F

Positive Identity

37. I feel I have control over things that happen to me.	T	F
38. I have a high self-esteem.	T	F
39. I believe my life has a purpose.	T	F
40. I am optimistic about my personal future.	T	F

BUILDING ASSETS, REDUCING RISKS

Developmental Assets among American Youth

Here are the percentages of sixth- to twelfth- graders surveyed by Search Institute who report having each asset. Compare your answers on the Assets Checklist to these results.

1. I receive lots of love and support from my family.	72%
2. My parent(s) and I communicate positively, and I am willing to go to my parent(s) for advice and counsel.	32%
3. I receive support from three or more nonparent adults.	50%
4. I experience caring neighbors.	40%
5. My school provides a caring, encouraging environment.	35%
6. My parent(s) are actively involved in helping me succeed in school.	33%
7. I believe that adults in the community value youth.	25%
8. I believe that young people are given useful roles in the community.	32%
9. I serve in my community for one hour or more per week.	50%
10. I feel safe at home, at school, and in the neighborhood.	54%
11. My family has clear rules and consequences, and monitors my whereabouts.	47%
12. My school provides clear rules and consequences.	56%
13. My neighbors take responsibility for monitoring young people's behavior.	48%
14. Parent(s) and other adults model positive, responsible behavior.	28%
15. My best friends model responsible behavior.	68%
16. Both my parent(s) and my teachers encourage me to do well.	55%
17. I spend three hours or more per week in sessions or practice in music, theater, or other arts.	20%
18. I spend three hours or more per week in sports, clubs, and organizations at school and/or in the community.	61%

1 of 2

111

19. I spend one or more hours per week in activities in a religious institution.	51%
20. I go with friends "with nothing special to do" two or fewer nights per week.	56%
21. I am motivated to do well in school.	71%
22. I am actively engaged in learning.	62%
23. I do at least one hour of homework every school day.	53%
24. I care about my school.	61%
25. I read for pleasure three or more hours per week.	23%
26. I place a high value on helping other people.	52%
27. I place a high value on promoting equality and reducing hunger and poverty.	54%
28. I act on my convictions and stand up for my beliefs.	71%
29. I tell the truth even when it is not easy.	69%
30. I accept and take personal responsibility.	67%
31. I believe it is important not to be sexually active or to use alcohol or other drugs.	47%
32. I know how to plan ahead and make choices.	33%
33. I have empathy, sensitivity, and friendship skills.	48%
34. I have knowledge of and comfort with people of different cultural/racial/ethnic backgrounds.	42%
35. I can resist negative peer pressure and dangerous situations.	45%
36. I seek to resolve conflict nonviolently.	44%
37. I feel I have control over things that happen to me.	45%
38. I have a high self-esteem.	52%
39. I believe my life has a purpose.	63%
40. I am optimistic about my personal future.	75%

2 of 2

BUILDING ASSETS, REDUCING RISKS

Assets by Grade and Gender

In the study of 89,366 youth nationwide, the number of assets youth experience by grade and gender are as follows:

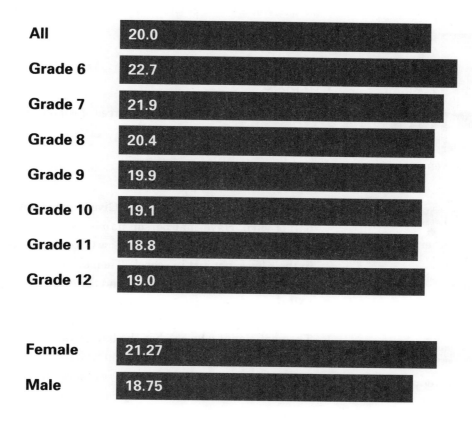

All	20.0
Grade 6	22.7
Grade 7	21.9
Grade 8	20.4
Grade 9	19.9
Grade 10	19.1
Grade 11	18.8
Grade 12	19.0
Female	21.27
Male	18.75

The number of assets youth experience was determined through the 2010 administration of the *Search Institute Profiles on Student Life: Attitudes and Behaviors* survey.

Session 23: Support Web

TIME NEEDED

• 30 minutes

ASSET CATEGORIES

• Support

RISK/PROTECTIVE FACTORS

• Opportunities for pro-social improvement

MATERIALS NEEDED

• A beach ball or other inflatable ball

• Yarn, enough to make a web

PREPARATION NEEDED

• Clear an area in your room so participants can sit in a circle.

Purpose

To help participants identify the sources of support in their lives

Instructions

1. Have participants sit in a circle. Give one participant a ball of yarn. Have that person name one person who supports him or her and, briefly, how (it could be anyone in their lives, not just in school). Then ask the participant to hold on to the end of the yarn and throw the rest of the ball to another person in the circle.

2. The participant who catches the ball of yarn then holds on to the yarn and names a person who supports him or her and how before throwing the rest of the ball of yarn to someone else. As the activity continues, a web that connects all the participants will appear. Make sure that everyone in the group gets to participate at least once.

3. After a web has been spun, explain that the ball represents young people and the web represents the web of support made up of all of the people mentioned.

4. Throw the beach ball into the web and encourage participants to move it around without letting it slip through the gaps in the web. If the web cannot support the ball, continue adding to it until the ball bounces easily without falling through.

5. Then stop and ask questions such as these:

- How many different types of people did we name (for example, family, friends, and neighbors)?

- Is it more important to you to have lots of different people who are supportive or just a few who are very supportive? Why?

- What happens when the gaps in our webs of support are too wide?

- Which attributes do supportive people have that are most important to you?

- In what ways do you support your friends and family?

- If someone you know seemed to need more support, how would you suggest that he or she find it?

Optional Follow-Up

Use the asset framework when discussing school and community issues.

Grades 6–8 Adaptations

Explain that the web represents a support system and each line of yarn represents a person. Younger participants may not understand the symbolism of the web, so a further explanation may be needed.

Session 24: Golden Nuggets

TIME NEEDED

- 30 minutes

ASSET CATEGORIES

- Empowerment

RISK/PROTECTIVE FACTORS

- Opportunities for pro-social involvement

MATERIALS NEEDED

- Rocks of different sizes, one per participant

PREPARATION NEEDED

- No preparation is needed

Purpose

- To help participants identify their own personal value and worth

- To recognize the importance of building internal assets

Instructions

1. Have participants sit in groups of four. Give each person a rock.

2. Instruct group members to compare their rocks and decide which rock is the most valuable and which is the least valuable. Then have group members arrange the rocks in a line that shows the order of value.

3. Ask groups to share how they determined which rocks were most valuable and why.

4. Then have participants pick up their original rocks. Tell them that each rock has gold inside, and each nugget of gold is unique. Have each group again arrange the rocks in a line that shows the order of value. This should be very difficult for them to do.

5. Ask questions such as these:

   - Was it more difficult to determine the value of the rocks based on what you could see on the outside or based on what you couldn't see on the inside? Why?

   - In terms of judging people, how do we usually decide who's valuable and who's not? Are those the best ways to determine value? Why or why not?

   - Think about all the age groups in our society. Which age groups are most valued? Least valued? Why?

   - Overall, how does our community do at valuing youth?

- Are youth in our community more likely to be viewed as valuable for what they are now or for what they might become?

- What would you suggest needs to happen to encourage our community to value youth more?

- What steps can you take to ensure that young people are valued?

Optional Follow-Up

Use the asset framework when discussing school and community issues.

Grades 6–8 Adaptations

No adaptations are needed.

Adapted with permission from Building Assets Together *by Jolene L. Roehlkepartain. Copyright © 1997 by Search Institute®, Minneapolis, MN; 800-888-7828; www.search-institute.org.*

Section 6: Grief and Loss

Session Title	Session Description	Materials Needed	Preparation Needed
Session 25: Grief and Loss	Through reviewing the handouts and a discussion, participants understand the process of grief and loss, exploring its impact on their lives.	• Stages of Grief packet • Exploring Anger handout	• Print and copy the Stages of Grief and Exploring Anger handouts, one per participant. • Invite the school social worker or school counselor to attend this session, optional.

BUILDING ASSETS, REDUCING RISKS

Duplicating this page is illegal. Do not duplicate without publisher's written permission.

119

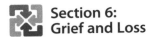
Session 25: Grief and Loss

- 30 minutes

- Social Competencies
- Support
- Positive Identity

- Increase in social skills

- Stages of Grief handout

- Exploring Anger handout

- Print and copy the two handouts, one copy per participant.
- Invite the school social worker or school counselor to attend this session, optional.

▶ **Facilitator note: IMPORTANT!** This session may arouse difficult feelings and memories for participants who have experienced a loss (such as death, divorce, or loss of a friend). If you are not comfortable facilitating the session alone, ask your school social worker or school counselor to co-facilitate, and be aware that some participants may need time to debrief after the session.

Purpose

- To understand the process of grief and loss
- To explore its impact on lives

Instructions

1. Distribute the Stages of Grief handout. Present the information in this handout to the group, stopping periodically to answer any questions.

2. Review each stage of grief using an example of losing your car keys.

   Example:

   - **Denial**—I've misplaced my car keys; I go to the drawer that I always keep them in and they are not there. I look in another drawer and I go back to the drawer that I keep them in and look again.

   - **Anger**—I slam the drawer. I stomp around the house; I swear; I yell.

   - **Bargaining**—I say to myself that if I find my car keys, I will always keep them in the same drawer.

   - **Sadness/Depression**—I start to feel sad because I'm going to be late and disappoint my friend because without my keys, I can't drive.

   - **Acceptance**—I realize the keys are not there, and I call someone to give me a ride.

3. Ask participants to form groups of two to four participants and discuss a situation in which they have experienced a change or loss (such as moving, divorce, changing schools, or death of a friend or relative).

4. Bring the large group back together and share the following information. It is important to understand the following:

   • Any loss involves going through these stages of grief.

   • People go through these stages in different ways.

   • There is no absolute order of the stages.

   • Everyone's timing is different as to how long they stay in a particular stage.

   • There is no way to rush through these stages.

   • It is always helpful to get support when going through change, loss, or grief.

5. Explain that the feeling of anger is very common during a loss or change. Distribute the Exploring Anger handout and talk through it with the whole group. Have participants share positive ways they have learned to handle anger.

Optional Follow-Up

Be aware of personal issues in participants' lives during the year. Review the stages of grief and loss with them, if needed.

Grades 6–8 Adaptations

When sharing change or loss in small groups, consider having an adult or older participant lead the discussion in each group.

Based on the Grief Cycle model, first published in On Death and Dying *by Elisabeth Kübler-Ross (New York: Scribner, 1969).*

Stages of Grief

Denial   Anger   Bargaining   Sadness/Depression   Acceptance

What Is Grief?

Grief occurs in response to the loss of someone or something. The loss may involve a loved one (death, divorce, abandonment, breakup), or a loss of a dream, or even loss of a role (a student leaving high school). Loss can occur as a surprise suddenly, or it can be expected. Grief is a normal and natural response to loss. It is important to realize and acknowledge that grief promotes healing following a loss.

Stages of Grief

There are five stages generally recognized as a part of the grieving process:

1. Denial

Denial is a normal defense mechanism that allows time to accept what is happening —similar to shock. Feelings associated with denial are often distancing, numbness, and/or withdrawal. An individual may show signs of denial by pretending the loss is not happening and/or pretending the loss doesn't matter.

2. Anger

Anger is a natural by-product of loss and can be overwhelming at times. Anger usually occurs when an individual feels helpless, powerless, and even abandoned.

3. Bargaining

Bargaining occurs when an individual becomes preoccupied about what he or she could have done to prevent the loss, or the ways things could have been better that will never be. If not properly resolved, bargaining may hinder the healing process.

4. Sadness/Depression

Depression can be a normal reaction to change and loss. Feelings of stress and sadness are a normal part of the grieving process. The following list of symptoms can be signs of depression:

1 of 2

- changes in eating or sleeping habits
- withdrawal or social isolation
- sudden changes in behavior
- acting-out behavior
- hyperactivity
- excessive self-criticism
- loss of interest or motivation
- psychosomatic complaints

- risk-taking behavior or self-destructive behavior
- accidents
- school problems
- sexual acting out
- suicidal talk or behavior

Down times are to be expected following a death or other loss, but sadness or anger that stays and doesn't go away may be a sign that help is needed.

5. Acceptance

At this point, change is no longer threatening and life has settled into a normal, if new, pattern. There can and should be optimism for the future. It is important to remember that changes will continue to happen and events can trigger old feelings of grief. The grieving process supports the individual. That is, healing occurs when the loss becomes integrated into the individual's life process.

Individuals experiencing grief may express their grief in a variety of ways. When talking about the stages of grief, it is helpful to recognize the following points:

- Grieving is a very fluid process—people may move back and forth between these stages before they reach the final stage of *acceptance*.

- People may experience the various stages of grief at different times and in different ways.

- There is no absolute order of experiencing the stages of grief.

When to Get Help

No matter how serious the loss, it is always helpful to talk about it with someone else—a friend, family member, or another trusted adult. Be sure to reach out and get help for yourself or a friend if

- the grief seems to get worse rather than better over time
- there is a change in personality or attitude
- the individual considers harming himself or herself or others

Exploring Anger

Anger is an important feeling. It motivates. It gives energy. It encourages assertiveness.

It's okay to feel angry. It's a natural human feeling that everyone experiences. But it's important to find healthy ways to express your anger. If not dealt with in a healthy way, anger can be harmful:

Physically

- Anger can hurt personally (headaches, rashes, ulcers, or stomachaches).
- Anger can hurt others (hitting, kicking, or throwing things).

Emotionally

- Anger can hurt personally (guilt, sadness, or depression).
- Anger can hurt others (putting others down, saying things that you later regret, or hurting feelings).

Relationships

- Anger can damage or destroy relationships.
- Communication can be blocked.
- Broken relationships can lead to being isolated and not being included.

Repressed Anger Can Be Very Harmful

Anger not dealt with can lead to other problems, such as alcohol and other drug use, health problems, violence, or relationship problems with family and friends.

Anger Has Three Parts—Thoughts, Feelings, and Actions

Thoughts trigger feelings and feelings trigger actions. It's okay to have angry thoughts and feelings. Everyone does. What is important is what a person does with the angry feelings.

1 of 2

Guidelines for Dealing with Anger

1. Recognize personal anger. Be able to say, "I'm angry." Accept it personally. Do not blame others for your anger.

2. Stop and think. Try to identify the reasons for your anger. What is making you angry? Are you understanding the situation correctly?

3. Decide if the situation is important. Is it worth being upset about?

4. Share it. Tell someone about the anger. Tell the person with whom you are angry, if this can be done without making the situation worse. Or talk to someone else who will listen.

5. Act on it in a positive way. (Punch a pillow, tear paper, run around the block, or write in a journal.)

6. Create a substitution. Try to find a more positive way of solving the problem, perhaps by making a compromise with the other person involved or by talking it out.

BUILDING ASSETS, REDUCING RISKS

Section 7: Bullying

Session Title	Session Description	Materials Needed	Preparation Needed
Session 26: Bullying	Through an activity, participants increase their awareness of bullying and their sensitivity to others.	• Index cards or paper, one per participant • Pens or pencils, one per participant	• None needed.

BUILDING ASSETS, REDUCING RISKS

Duplicating this page is illegal. Do not duplicate without publisher's written permission.

127

Session 26: Bullying

TIME NEEDED

• 30 minutes

ASSET CATEGORIES

• Support

• Social Competencies

• Positive Values

• Positive Identity

RISK/PROTECTIVE FACTORS

• Increase in social skills

MATERIALS NEEDED

• Index cards or blank
  sheets of paper,
  one per participant

• Pens or pencils,
  one per participant

PREPARATION NEEDED

• No preparation is
  needed.

Purpose

• To raise awareness of bullying

• To increase participants' sensitivity toward others

Instructions

1. Ask participants to think of someone they feel has been
   bullied. (This is a confidential activity; participants can
   think of themselves too.) If participants need a definition
   of bullying, explain that bullying is when someone
   repeatedly and on purpose says or does mean or hurtful
   things to another person who has a hard time defending
   himself or herself.

2. Ask participants to stand in a single, straight line. If
   space doesn't allow for participants to form a single line,
   have them complete the activity by standing next to their
   desks instead of stepping forward.

3. This activity should be done in complete silence. Explain
   that a series of statements will be read aloud. If the
   statement is true for the person they are thinking about,
   participants should step forward. Let participants know if
   the statement applies to the person they are thinking of,
   but they don't feel comfortable stepping forward, that is
   fine. Participants should note their feelings in response to
   each statement that is read.

4. Ask participants to notice who stepped forward and who
   didn't. Remind participants there is no talking.

5. Ask all participants to silently think about how it feels to
   take a step. Notice how it feels to watch others take a step.
   Ask participants to return to their original place before
   reading the next statement.

Here are the statements that should be read one at a time:

- Take a step if your person has ever seen someone else being teased or called a bad name.

- Take a step if your person has ever been teased or called a bad name.

- Take a step if your person has ever been teased about her or his voice (having an accent or being told you can't sing, for example).

- Take a step if your person or any member of your person's family has a disability.

- Take a step if your person has been kicked, pushed, or shoved around.

- Take a step if your person has been whistled at or harassed in a sexual way.

- Take a step if your person has been picked last for games or sports, or not included at all.

- Take a step if your person has been put down or discriminated against because of his or her skin color.

- Take a step if your person has been put down or discriminated against because of his or her sexual orientation or suspected sexual orientation.

- Take a step if your person has ever been teased about wearing glasses, wearing hearing aids, the style of his or her clothes, or the shape of his or her body.

6. Ask the participants to form pairs or small groups and to discuss the following questions and brainstorm a list of answers:

- What can someone do if they see a person being bullied?

- What can someone do if they themselves are being bullied?

- What should the adults in school do if a student is being bullied?

BUILDING ASSETS, REDUCING RISKS
Duplicating this page is illegal. Do not duplicate without publisher's written permission.

129

7. Reconvene the large group. If time permits, invite the participants to share their ideas from their small groups.

8. Read the following to all participants:

- It takes courage to take a step. It takes courage to recognize and stand up against bullying. Differences are sometimes used to justify bullying in our society. Everyone knows what it is like to be hurt, or to see someone hurt, and not stand up for them. It is important to remember what we shared here today, how it made us feel, and try to ensure that no one gets hurt in these ways again.

9. Give an index card and a pen or pencil to each participant. Ask participants to consider how they could be of support to someone who is being bullied and to then write on their index card a commitment of how they can support students who are being bullied. Remind participants that sometimes the best way to provide support is to tell an adult and ask for help.

Optional Follow-Up

In one month, ask participants to remember what they wrote on their cards. Ask if they have been able to keep their commitments.

Grades 6–8 Adaptations

No adaptations are needed.

NOTES

Section 8: Diversity

Session Title	Session Description	Materials Needed	Preparation Needed
Session 27: Values	Through a survey and discussion, participants understand their own values and the values of others.	• Values Survey handout • Pens or pencils, one per participant	• Print and copy the Values Survey handout, one per participant.
Session 28: Fishbowls	Through communication, participants understand how gender roles affect their lives.	• Chairs, one per participant	• Move chairs into a circle.
Session 29: Taking the Human Rights Temperature of Your School	Through a questionnaire and discussion, participants identify strengths and areas of needed improvements in their school.	• Human Rights Packet • Pens or pencils, one per participant • Whiteboard or Smart Board • Marker	• Print and copy the Human Rights Packet, one per participant.

BUILDING ASSETS, REDUCING RISKS

Duplicating this page is illegal. Do not duplicate without publisher's written permission.

131

 **Section 8: Diversity**

Classroom Curriculum, Volume 1

Session 27: Values

- 30 minutes

- Social Competencies
- Positive Values
- Positive Identity

RISK/PROTECTIVE FACTORS

- Increase in social skills

- The Values Survey handout 27-1
- Pens or pencils, one per participant

- Print and copy the Values Survey handout, one per participant.

Purpose

To help participants understand their own values and the values of others

Instructions

1. Distribute the Values Survey handout and a pen or pencil to each participant. Ask participants to complete the survey individually.

2. Explain that what they listed as most important are the things they "value" the most. Our values are the things we hold most important. Sometimes the things we value are external, such as a good job or a nice car. Sometimes the things we value are internal, such as honesty, integrity, and peace of mind.

3. Ask participants to form groups of two to four participants. Group members should take turns sharing their list of important things, then discuss the following questions:

   - How do values influence our behavior?

   - How do you determine which values are right for you?

   - Do others use the same criteria as you in establishing values?

   - Can you respect a value you don't agree with?

4. Reconvene the large group, asking small groups to share highlights from their discussion of the questions.

BUILDING ASSETS, REDUCING RISKS

132

Duplicating this page is illegal. Do not duplicate without publisher's written permission.

Optional Follow-Up

Remind participants of their values when reviewing goals or developing dreams.

Grades 6–8 Adaptations

Younger participants may have more difficulty identifying and discussing their personal values. Plan to skip the small group discussions and hold a large group discussion instead.

Values Survey

Think about what you value in life and then list the
following items in order of importance:

Items

Fame

Close friends

Money

Peace with self

Car

Respect

God

Large home

Loving family

High-paying job

Others not listed:

_____

_____

_____

My List by Importance

_____

_____

_____

_____

_____

_____

_____

_____

_____

_____

_____

_____

_____

Explain why the first two items you listed are important to you.

Item 1: _____

Item 2: _____

Session 28: Fishbowls

TIME NEEDED

• 30 minutes

ASSET CATEGORIES

• Positive Identity
• Support
• Positive Values

RISK/PROTECTIVE FACTORS

• Increase in social skills

MATERIALS NEEDED

• Chairs, one per
  participant based on
  gender—girls will
  sit first, then boys

PREPARATION NEEDED

• Move the chairs
  into a circle.

Purpose

To help participants understand how gender roles affect
their lives

Instructions

1. Ask all female participants to sit in a chair in the circle.

2. Ask each of the males to stand behind a chair outside the
   circle and be a silent observer. Be sure these participants
   are respectful of the discussion that will be happening.

3. Ask female participants to discuss what it is like growing
   up female. Allow ten minutes for discussion. Here are
   some possible questions to guide the discussion:

   • What are the advantages to growing up female?

   • What are the disadvantages to growing up female?

   • What do you think are the advantages to growing
     up male?

   • What do you think are the disadvantages to growing
     up male?

4. After ten minutes, ask the male participants their
   thoughts and feelings about the discussion. Were there
   any surprises? (Make sure the male participants don't
   ridicule or make fun of the female participants.)

5. Reverse roles by having the male participants sit in the
   chairs with the female participants standing behind the
   chairs as silent observers. Again, be sure the observers
   are respectful of the discussion that will be happening.

BUILDING ASSETS, REDUCING RISKS
Duplicating this page is illegal. Do not duplicate without publisher's written permission.

135

6. Ask male participants to discuss what it is like growing up male. Allow ten minutes for discussion. Here are some possible questions to guide the discussion:

   • What are the advantages to growing up male?

   • What are the disadvantages to growing up male?

   • What do you think are the advantages to growing up female?

   • What do you think are the disadvantages to growing up female?

7. After ten minutes, ask the female participants their thoughts and feelings about the discussion. Were there any surprises? (Again, make sure the female participants don't ridicule or make fun of the male participants.)

8. Reconvene the large group and lead a discussion using the following questions:

   • How does being female or male influence your behavior? How does being female or male influence your daily life?

   • How does gender influence the decisions you make?

Optional Follow-Up

Identify times gender roles are influencing behavior in school and in society.

Grades 6–8 Adaptations

Adapt this activity if appropriate for your participants' grade and maturity level. Very young participants may have difficulty answering the questions. Perhaps focus more on concrete differences, such as differences in household chores, interests, or childhood experiences.

Session 29: Taking the Human Rights Temperature of Your School

TIME NEEDED

• 30 minutes

ASSET CATEGORIES

• Social Competencies

• Empowerment

RISK/PROTECTIVE FACTORS

• Bonding and attachment to schools

MATERIALS NEEDED

• Human Rights Packet

• Pens or pencils, one per participant

• Whiteboard or Smart Board

• Marker

PREPARATION NEEDED

• Print and copy the Human Rights Packet, one per participant.

Purpose

To help participants identify strengths and areas of needed improvements in their school

Instructions

1. Distribute the Human Rights Packet and a pen or pencil to each participant.

2. Read aloud the Taking the Human Rights Temperature of Your School document in the Human Rights Packet. Share your views on what human rights look like within a school environment.

3. Ask participants to complete the Human Rights Questionnaire.

4. Ask participants to form groups of two to four participants to discuss their responses to the questionnaire.

5. Return to the large group and discuss the following questions:

   • Is our school a place where everyone feels safe and secure?

   • Are we accommodating every student's needs?

   • How do we resolve conflicts in our school?

   • Does our school welcome people from diverse backgrounds?

6. Conclude the discussion with these questions:

   • How might we improve our school's human rights climate? (Write suggestions on the whiteboard or Smart Board.)

   • Would you be willing to make a commitment to improve our school based on the ideas you listed?

BUILDING ASSETS, REDUCING RISKS
Duplicating this page is illegal. Do not duplicate without publisher's written permission.

137

7. Ask participants to make a commitment to improve the school's human rights climate.

Optional Follow-Up

Encourage participants to be aware of their school's human rights issues.

Grades 6–8 Adaptations

- Talk about how human rights apply to your specific school.

- Change the Human Rights Questionnaire so that the answers are yes or no.

- Offer examples of ideas to improve the school's human rights climate, encouraging participants to generate their own ideas.

- For a lower grade level, break this activity into three separate sessions: talking about human rights in general, human rights at a school, and personal human rights. With each session, talk about what people are currently doing to improve human rights, and then ask participants to think of new ideas on how to improve human rights.

Used with permission from: D. Shiman and K. Rudelius-Palmer, Economic and Social Justice: A Human Rights Perspective (Minneapolis: Human Rights Resource Center, University of Minnesota, 1999), www.hrusa.org/hrmaterials/temperature.

Human Rights Packet

Taking the Human Rights Temperature of Your School

Introduction

The questions in the Human Rights Questionnaire on the following pages are adapted from the United Nations Universal Declaration of Human Rights (UDHR). The relevant UDHR articles are included parenthetically in each statement. Some of these issues correlate more directly to the UDHR than others. All of these questions are related to the fundamental human right to education found in Article 26 of the Universal Declaration. It asserts:

> *Everyone has the right to education . . . Education shall be directed to the full development of the human personality and to the strengthening of respect for human rights and fundamental freedoms.*

When discrimination is mentioned in the questionnaire it refers to a wide range of conditions: race, ethnicity or culture, sex, physical or intellectual capacities, friendship associations, age, culture, disability, social class or financial status, physical appearance, sexual orientation, lifestyle choices, nationality, and living space. Although this is a much more expansive list than that found in the Universal Declaration of Human Rights, it is more helpful in assessing the human rights temperature in your school community.

The results should provide a general sense of the school's climate in light of principles found in the Universal Declaration of Human Rights. Obviously, more questions are needed and follow-up questioning during the discussion will enrich the assessment. These questions can help to identify specific areas of concern that need to be addressed.

Human Rights Questionnaire

Directions

To assess the human rights temperature of our school, read each statement and assess how accurately it describes our school community. Record a score in the blank next to each statement. Use the scale of 1–4, as described below, for scoring. Keep in mind all members of our school: students, teachers, administrators, and other staff. Add all numbers together to determine the overall assessment score for our school.

1 = no/never   2 = rarely   3 = often   4 = yes/always

_____ 1. My school is a place where students are safe and secure. (Articles 3 and 5)

_____ 2. All students receive equal information and encouragement about academic and career opportunities. (Article 2)

_____ 3. Members of the school community are not discriminated against because of their lifestyle choices, such as manner of dress, association with certain people, and non-school activities. (Articles 2 and 16)

_____ 4. My school provides equal access, resources, activities, and scheduling accommodations for all individuals. (Articles 2 and 7)

_____ 5. Members of my school community oppose discriminatory or demeaning actions, materials, or slurs in the school. (Articles 2, 3, 7, 28, and 29)

_____ 6. When someone demeans or violates the rights of another person, the violator is helped to learn how to change his or her behavior. (Article 26)

_____ 7. Members of my school community care about my full human as well as my academic development and try to help me when I am in need. (Articles 3, 22, 26, and 29)

_____ 8. When conflicts arise, we try to resolve them through nonviolent ways. (Articles 3 and 28)

_____ 9. Institutional policies and procedures are implemented when complaints of harassment or discrimination are submitted. (Articles 3 and 7)

Human Rights Questionnaire *continued*

1 = no/never   2 = rarely   3 = often   4 = yes/always

_____ 10. In matters related to discipline (including suspension and expulsion), all persons are assured of fair, impartial treatment in the determination of guilt and assignment of punishment. (Articles 6, 7, 8, 9, and 10)

_____ 11. No one in my school is subjected to degrading treatment or punishment. (Article 5)

_____ 12. Someone accused of wrongdoing is presumed innocent until proven guilty. (Article 11)

_____ 13. My personal space and possessions are respected. (Articles 12 and 17)

_____ 14. My school community welcomes students, teachers, administrators, and staff from diverse backgrounds and cultures, including people not born in the United States. (Articles 2, 6, 13, 14, and 15)

_____ 15. I have the liberty to express my beliefs and ideas (political, religious, cultural, or other) without fear of discrimination. (Article 19)

_____ 16. Members of my school can produce and disseminate publications without fear of censorship or punishment. (Article 19)

_____ 17. Diverse voices and perspectives (such as gender, race/ethnicity, and ideological) are represented in courses, textbooks, assemblies, libraries, and classroom instruction. (Articles 2, 19, and 27)

_____ 18. I have the opportunity to express my culture through music, art, and literary forms. (Articles 19, 27, and 28)

_____ 19. Members of my school have the opportunity to participate (individually and through associations) in democratic decision-making processes to develop school policies and rules. (Articles 20, 21, and 23)

_____ 20. Members of my school have the right to form associations within the school to advocate for their rights or the rights of others. (Articles 19, 20, and 23)

_____ 21. Members of my school encourage each other to learn about societal and global problems related to justice, ecology, poverty, and peace. (Preamble and Articles 26 and 29)

3 of 11

Human Rights Questionnaire *continued*

1 = no/never   2 = rarely   3 = often   4 = yes/always

_____ 22. Members of my school encourage each other to organize and take action to address societal and global problems related to justice, ecology, poverty, and peace. (Preamble and Articles 20 and 29)

_____ 23. Members of my school community are able to take adequate rest or recess time during the school day and work reasonable hours under fair work conditions. (Articles 23 and 24)

_____ 24. Employees in my school are paid enough to have a standard of living adequate for the health and well-being (including housing, food, necessary social services, and security from unemployment, sickness, and old age) of themselves and their families. (Articles 22 and 25)

_____ 25. I take responsibility in my school to ensure that other individuals do not discriminate and behave in ways that promote the safety and well-being of my school community. (Articles 1 and 29)

Temperature possible = 100 Human Rights Degrees

Add all numbers together to determine the overall assessment score.

Your school's temperature: _____

Source: Adapted from David Shiman, *Teaching Human Rights* (Denver: Center for Teaching International Relations, University of Denver, 1999). Written with Kristi Rudelius-Palmer.

Dimensions of Racism

Lack of information: "ignorance."
People act or speak from a place or position that indicates that they have not learned about the other person's culture. They are well meaning but often are unaware that they have offended or alienated the other person.

Lack of sensitivity: "insensitivity."
People are aware of the differences of culture or may know that they have offended someone but choose to disregard the offended person's feelings or believe they don't have to respond to that person's feelings. They are not hateful but often hold stereotypical beliefs and attitudes, and/or refuse to listen and learn from others.

Intentional racism: "racism."
People believe that one group is better than another. They hold on to beliefs that are negative and destructive and often believe that they need to separate themselves from people who are different. In extreme cases, they believe they need to punish people who are different from them through hate crimes.

Institutional racism:
Organizations or systems intentionally or unintentionally maintain and support the dominant culture. Many times these systems and the people within them are not aware of the level of discomfort for people from other cultures. Sometimes these systems are so closed they keep people from joining or feeling a part of the whole through rules or expectations.

Source: Adapted from the Diversity Program at Headway Emotional Health Services (formerly the Storefront Group), 6425 Nicollet Avenue South, Richfield, Minnesota, www.headway.org.

Universal Declaration of Human Rights (UDHR)

PREAMBLE

Whereas recognition of the inherent dignity and of the equal and inalienable rights of all members of the human family is the foundation of freedom, justice and peace in the world,

Whereas disregard and contempt for human rights have resulted in barbarous acts which have outraged the conscience of mankind, and the advent of a world in which human beings shall enjoy freedom of speech and belief and freedom from fear and want has been proclaimed as the highest aspiration of the common people,

Whereas it is essential, if man is not to be compelled to have recourse, as a last resort, to rebellion against tyranny and oppression, that human rights should be protected by the rule of law,

Whereas the peoples of the United Nations have in the Charter reaffirmed their faith in fundamental human rights in the dignity and worth of the human person and in the equal rights of men and women and have determined to promote social progress and better standards of life in larger freedom,

Whereas Member States pledged themselves to achieve, in cooperation with the United Nations, the promotion of universal respect for and observance of human rights and fundamental freedoms,

Whereas a common understanding of these rights and freedoms is of the greatest importance for the full realization of this pledge.

Now, therefore,

THE GENERAL ASSEMBLY

Proclaims this Universal Declaration of Human Rights as a common standard of achievement for all peoples and all nations, to the end that every individual and every organ of society, keeping this Declaration constantly in mind, shall strive by teaching and education to promote respect for these rights and freedoms and by progressive measure, national and international, to secure her or his universal and effective recognition and observance, both among the peoples of Member States themselves and among the peoples of territories under their jurisdiction.

Article 1

All human beings are born free and equal in dignity and rights. They are endowed with reason and conscience and should act towards one another in a spirit of brotherhood.

Article 2

Everyone is entitled to all the rights and freedoms set forth in this Declaration without distinction of any kind, such as race, color, sex, language, religion, political or other opinion, national or social origin, property, birth or other status.

Furthermore, no distinction shall be made on the basis of the political, jurisdictional or international status of the country or territory to which a person belongs, whether it be independent, trust, non-self-governing or under any other limitation of sovereignty.

Article 3

Everyone has the right to life, liberty and security of person.

UDHR *continued*

Article 4

No one shall be held in slavery or servitude; slavery and the slave trade shall be prohibited in all their forms.

Article 5

No one shall be subjected to torture or to cruel, inhuman or degrading treatment or punishment.

Article 6

Everyone has the right to recognition everywhere as a person before the law.

Article 7

All are equal before the law and are entitled without any discrimination to equal protection of the law. All are entitled to equal protection against any discrimination in violation of the Declaration and against any incitement to such discrimination.

Article 8

Everyone has the right to an effective remedy by the competent national tribunals for acts violating the fundamental rights granted him by the constitution or by law.

Article 9

No one shall be subjected to arbitrary arrest, detention or exile.

Article 10

Everyone is entitled in full equality to a fair and public hearing by an independent and impartial tribunal, in the determination of his rights and obligations and of any criminal charge against him.

Article 11

Everyone charged with a penal offense has the right to be presumed innocent until proved guilty according to law in a public trial at which he has had all the guarantees necessary for his defense.

No one shall be held guilty of any penal offense on account of any act or omission which did not constitute a penal offense, under national or international law, at the time when it was committed. Nor shall a heavier penalty be imposed than the one that was applicable at the time the penal offense was committed.

Article 12

No one shall be subjected to arbitrary interference with his privacy, family, home or correspondence, nor to attacks upon his honor and reputation. Everyone has the right to the protection of the law against such interference or attacks.

Article 13

1. Everyone has the right to freedom of movement and residence within the borders of each state.

2. Everyone has the right to leave any country, including his own, and to return to his country.

Article 14

1. Everyone has the right to seek and to enjoy in other countries asylum from persecution.

2. This right may not be invoked in the case of prosecutions genuinely arising from non-political crimes or from acts contrary to the purposes and principles of the United Nations.

Article 15

1. Everyone has the right to a nationality.

2. No one shall be arbitrarily deprived of his nationality nor denied the right to change his nationality.

UDHR *continued*

Article 16

1. Men and women of full age, without any limitation due to race, nationality or religion, have the right to marry and to found a family. They are entitled to equal rights as to marriage, during marriage and at its dissolution.

2. Marriage shall be entered into only with the free and full consent of the intending spouses.

3. The family is the natural and fundamental group unit of society and is entitled to protection by society and the State.

Article 17

1. Everyone has the right to own property alone as well as in association with others.

2. No one shall be arbitrarily deprived of his property.

Article 18

Everyone has the right to freedom of thought, conscience and religion; this right includes freedom to change his religion or belief, and freedom, either alone or in community with others and in public or private, to manifest his religion or belief in teaching practice, worship and observance.

Article 19

Everyone has the right to freedom of opinion and expression; this right includes freedom to hold opinions without interference and to seek, receive and impart information and ideas through any media and regardless of frontiers.

Article 20

1. Everyone has the right to freedom of peaceful assembly and association.

2. No one may be compelled to belong to an association.

Article 21

1. Everyone has the right to take part in the government of his country, directly or through freely chosen representatives.

2. Everyone has the right of equal access to public service in his country.

3. The will of the people shall be the basis of the authority of government; this will shall be expressed in periodic and genuine elections which shall be by universal and equal suffrage and shall be held by secret vote or by equivalent free voting procedures.

Article 22

Everyone, as a member of society, has the right to social security and is entitled to realization, through national effort and international cooperation and in accordance with the organization and resources of each State, of the economic, social and cultural rights indispensable for this dignity and the free development of his personality.

Article 23

1. Everyone has the right to work, to free choice of employment, to just and favorable conditions of work and to protection against unemployment.

2. Everyone, without any discrimination, has the right to equal pay for equal work.

3. Everyone who works has the right to just and favorable remuneration ensuring for himself and his family an existence worthy of human dignity, and supplemented, if necessary, by other means of social protection.

4. Everyone has the right to form and to join trade unions for the protection of his interests.

8 of 11

UDHR *continued*

Article 24

Everyone has the right to rest and leisure, including reasonable limitation of working hours and periodic holidays with pay.

Article 25

1. Everyone has the right to a standard of living adequate for the health and well-being of himself and of his family, including food, clothing, housing and medical care and necessary social services, and the right to security in the event of unemployment, sickness, disability, widowhood, old age or other lack of livelihood in circumstances beyond his control.

2. Motherhood and childhood are entitled to special care and assistance. All children, whether born in or out of wedlock, shall enjoy the same social protection.

Article 26

1. Everyone has the right to education. Education shall be free, at least in the elementary and fundamental stages. Elementary education shall be compulsory. Technical and professional education shall be made generally available and higher education shall be equally accessible to all on the basis of merit.

2. Education shall be directed to the full development of the human personality and to the strengthening of respect for human rights and fundamental freedoms. It shall promote understanding, tolerance and friendship among all Nations, racial or religious groups, and shall further the activities of the United Nations for the maintenance of peace.

3. Parents have a prior right to choose the kind of education that shall be given to their children.

Article 27

1. Everyone has the right freely to participate in the cultural life of the community, to enjoy the arts and to share in scientific advancement and its benefits.

2. Everyone has the right to the protection of the moral and material interests resulting from any scientific, literary or artistic production of which he is the author.

Article 28

Everyone is entitled to a social and international order in which the rights and freedoms set forth in this Declaration can be fully realized.

Article 29

1. Everyone has duties to the community in which alone the free and full development of his personality is possible.

2. In the exercise of his rights and freedoms, everyone shall be subject only to such limitations as are determined by law solely for the purpose of securing due recognition and respect for the rights and freedoms of others and of meeting the just requirements of morality, public order and the general welfare in a democratic society.

3. These rights and freedoms may in no case be exercised contrary to the purposes and principles of the United Nations.

Article 30

Nothing in the Declaration may be interpreted as implying for any State, group or person any right to engage in any activity or to perform any act aimed at the destruction of any of the rights and freedoms set forth herein.

9 of 11

147

Universal Declaration of Human Rights (Abbreviated)

Article 1
Right to Equality

Article 2
Freedom from Discrimination

Article 3
Right to Life, Liberty, Personal Security

Article 4
Freedom from Slavery

Article 5
Freedom from Torture and Degrading
Treatment

Article 6
Right to Recognition as a Person before
the Law

Article 7
Right to Equality before the Law

Article 8
Right to Remedy by Competent Tribunal

Article 9
Freedom from Arbitrary Arrest and Exile

Article 10
Right to Fair Public Hearing

Article 11
Right to Be Considered Innocent until
Proven Guilty

Article 12
Freedom from Interference with Privacy,
Family, Home and Correspondence

Article 13
Right to Free Movement in and out of
the Country

Article 14
Right to Asylum in Other Countries from
Persecution

Article 15
Right to a Nationality and the Freedom
to Change It

Article 16
Right to Marriage and Family

Article 17
Right to Own Property

Article 18
Freedom of Belief and Religion

Article 19
Freedom of Opinion and Information

Article 20
Right of Peaceful Assembly and Association

Article 21
Right to Participate in Government and in
Free Elections

Article 22
Right to Social Security

Article 23
Right to Desirable Work and to Join Trade
Unions

Article 24
Right to Rest and Leisure

Article 25
Right to Adequate Living Standard

Article 26
Right to Education

Article 27
Right to Participate in the Cultural Life of
Community

Article 28
Right to a Social Order that Articulates this
Document

Article 29
Community Duties Essential to Free and Full
Development

Article 30
Freedom from State or Personal Interference
in the above Rights

Personal Rights

You have:

The right to act in ways that promote your dignity and self-respect as long as others' rights are not violated in the process.

1. The right to be treated with respect

2. The right to say no and not feel guilty

3. The right to experience and express your feelings

4. The right to take time to slow down and think

5. The right to change your mind

6. The right to ask for what you want

7. The right to do less than you are humanly capable of doing

8. The right to ask for information

9. The right to make mistakes

10. The right to feel good about yourself

Section 9: Risky Behavior

Session Title	Session Description	Materials Needed	Preparation Needed
Session 30: Risky Behavior	Through completing a handout and discussion, participants recognize high-risk behaviors.	• Health-Compromising Risk-Taking handout • Pens or pencils, one per participant • Whiteboard or Smart Board • Markers	• Print and copy the Health-Compromising Risk-Taking handout, one per participant.
Session 31: Risky Behavior Skit	Through creating and performing a skit, participants recognize health-compromising risky behaviors and produce a list of positive alternatives.	• List of health-compromising risks from session 30	• None needed.
Session 32: Substance Use	Through this exercise, participants recognize what a substance use disorder is and learn about substances.	• Substance Use Disorder Definitions handout • Recognizing a Substance Use Disorder (two pages) • Pens or pencils, one for every four participants	• Print and copy the Substance Use Disorder Definitions and Recognizing a Substance Use Disorder handouts, one per participant.
Session 33: Enabling	Through completing a handout and discussion, participants understand enabling, which is defined as anything a person does that causes someone's alcohol or other drug use to continue or get worse.	• Understanding Enabling handout • Understanding Enabling Answer Key • Pens or pencils, one per participant	• Print and copy Understanding Enabling handout, one per participant.
Session 34: Circles of Support	Through this activity and discussion, participants identify and recognize the importance of circles of support.	• Post-it Notes, two per participant • Pens or pencils, one per participant	• Set out Post-it Notes and pens or pencils.

BUILDING ASSETS, REDUCING RISKS

Duplicating this page is illegal. Do not duplicate without publisher's written permission.

151

Session 30: Risky Behavior

TIME NEEDED

• 30 minutes

ASSET CATEGORIES

• Social Competencies

• Boundaries and
Expectations

• Positive Values

RISK/PROTECTIVE FACTORS

• Increase in social skills

MATERIALS NEEDED

• Health-
Compromising
Risk-Taking
handout

• Pens or pencils, one
per participant

• Whiteboard or
Smart Board

• Markers

PREPARATION NEEDED

• Print and copy the
Health-Compromising
Risk-Taking handout,
one per participant.

Purpose

To recognize high-risk behavior

Instructions

1. Ask: "When you hear the term 'risk-taking,' what does
   that mean to you?" Allow time for participant responses.

2. Discuss the following:

   • Everyone takes risks. We take risks when we ride a
     bike, audition for a play, try out for a team, raise our
     hand to answer a question, or try a new activity. Adults
     also take risks when they choose a career, buy a home,
     or apply for a new job. Risk-taking is part of growing
     up—a part of maturing and a part of life.

3. Ask participants to brainstorm healthy risks. Record the
   responses on the whiteboard or Smart Board.

4. Discuss health-compromising risks:

   • There are risks people take that can compromise their
     health, for example, not wearing a helmet when riding
     a bike or not exercising. What other kinds of activities
     might be compromising one's health?

   Record responses on the whiteboard or Smart Board, and
   save the responses for next week's activity.

5. Distribute the Health-Compromising Risk-Taking handout
   and a pen or pencil to each participant. Ask participants
   to complete the handout individually.

6. Divide into small groups of three to four people. Ask participants to compare their answers on the Health-Compromising Risk-Taking handout. Ask group members to determine what makes a behavior risky or not risky. Ask a representative from each group to write the group's conclusions on the back of her or his handout.

7. Return to the large group and ask a representative from each group to report the results of their discussion. Write their responses on the whiteboard or Smart Board.

Optional Follow-Up

Throughout the year, remind participants of healthy and unhealthy risk-taking behavior.

Grades 6-8 Adaptations

No adaptations are needed.

BUILDING ASSETS, REDUCING RISKS

Duplicating this page is illegal. Do not duplicate without publisher's written permission.

153

Health-Compromising Risk-Taking

Circle how risky you think the following behaviors are, using a scale of 1–5.

Is This a Risky Behavior?	Not Very Risky ⟷ Very Risky				
Not exercising regularly	1	2	3	4	5
Eating junk food	1	2	3	4	5
Skipping class once	1	2	3	4	5
Skipping class regularly	1	2	3	4	5
Not wearing a helmet when riding a bike	1	2	3	4	5
Not wearing a seatbelt while riding in a car	1	2	3	4	5
Exceeding the speed limit while driving	1	2	3	4	5
Smoking one or two cigarettes	1	2	3	4	5
Smoking one or two cigarettes per day	1	2	3	4	5
Drinking alcohol with your parents	1	2	3	4	5
Drinking alcohol with your friends	1	2	3	4	5
Visiting a chat room on the Internet	1	2	3	4	5
Spending two hours a day in a chat room on the Internet	1	2	3	4	5
Going on a crash diet	1	2	3	4	5
Taking diet pills to lose weight	1	2	3	4	5
Walking alone at night	1	2	3	4	5
Having sexual intercourse	1	2	3	4	5
Drinking alcohol and driving	1	2	3	4	5
Smoking marijuana	1	2	3	4	5

BUILDING ASSETS, REDUCING RISKS

Session 31: Risky Behavior Skit

TIME NEEDED

• 30 minutes

ASSET CATEGORIES

• Social Competencies

• Boundaries and Expectations

• Positive Values

RISK/PROTECTIVE FACTORS

• Increase in social skills

MATERIALS NEEDED

• List of risky, health-compromising behaviors from the last session's activity

PREPARATION NEEDED

• No preparation is needed.

Purpose

• To recognize health-compromising risky behaviors

• To develop a list of positive alternatives for those behaviors

Instructions

1. Divide the participants into small groups of three to four people.

2. Ask each group to select a risky behavior (possibly from the list generated in the last session) and create a skit that demonstrates the behavior, the potential consequences of that behavior, and a positive alternative behavior. The skit may be in the form of a play, a commercial, or an educational announcement. Remind participants that all skits need to be appropriate and in good taste. Skits should be a few minutes long. Groups will have ten minutes to work on the skit.

3. Ask each small group to perform its skit for the large group.

4. Following each skit, discuss the following questions with the large group:

   • What was the risky behavior that was being demonstrated?

   • Will the proposed alternative work to avoid the risky behavior?

   • Do you have additional ideas for alternatives?

BUILDING ASSETS, REDUCING RISKS

Duplicating this page is illegal. Do not duplicate without publisher's written permission.

155

Optional Follow-Up

Remind participants of this activity and alternatives to risky behaviors throughout the year.

Grades 6–8 Adaptations

No adaptations are needed.

Session 32: Substance Use

TIME NEEDED

• 30 minutes

Purpose

• To recognize a substance use disorder

• To learn about substances

ASSET CATEGORIES

• Boundaries and
  Expectations

• Social Competencies

RISK/PROTECTIVE FACTORS

• Knowledge of substance
  use

MATERIALS NEEDED

• Substance Use
  Disorder Definitions
  handout

• Recognizing a
  Substance Use
  Disorder handout

• Pens or pencils, one for
  every four participants

PREPARATION NEEDED

• Print and copy the
  Substance Use Disorder
  Definitions and
  Recognizing a Substance
  Use Disorder handouts,
  one per participant.

Instructions

1. Native American culture has a rich history filled with
   oral traditions. There is a Cherokee legend called "The
   Little Boy and the Rattlesnake," which does a brilliant
   job explaining the risks of substance use. Please read
   the legend aloud to participants.

   **Wait to read the moral until after the group
   discussion** (see page 159).

2. Discuss the reading with participants:

   • How does the story of the American Indian youth
     relate to substance use?

   • What lesson did the young American Indian learn?

   • What is the meaning of the statement "You knew
     what I was when you picked me up"?

3. Distribute the Substance Use Disorder Definitions
   handout. In the large group, describe and discuss what
   a substance use disorder is and other related definitions
   on the handout.

4. Distribute the Recognizing a Substance Use Disorder
   handout to each participant. Talk through each of the
   levels and how they relate to the definition of a substance
   use disorder.

5. Divide participants into small groups of four to six people
   and give a pen or pencil to each group. Discreetly assign
   one level of substance use to each group. Make sure all
   five levels have been distributed among the small groups.
   Ask each group to complete the Recognizing a Substance
   Use Disorder exercise using the assigned level.

BUILDING ASSETS, REDUCING RISKS

Duplicating this page is illegal. Do not duplicate without publisher's written permission.

157

6. Reconvene as a large group and ask a representative from each group to share their small group responses with the large group. Ask participants in the large group to guess which level of substance use is being described.

Optional Follow-Up

Encourage participants to be aware of any substance use by their friends. Remind participants of the story of the American Indian youth and encourage them to apply the story to their lives. Ask, "How does the statement, 'You knew what I was when you picked me up' apply in your personal life?"

Grades 6–8 Adaptations

Explain and discuss the true meaning of "The Little Boy and the Rattlesnake" story before moving on to the questions.

The Little Boy and the Rattlesnake

Many years ago, American Indian youth would go away in solitude to prepare for manhood. One such youth hiked into a beautiful valley, green with trees, bright with flowers. There he fasted. But on the third day, as he looked up at the surrounding mountains, he noticed one tall rugged peak, capped with dazzling snow.

I will test myself against that mountain, he thought. He put on his buffalo-hide shirt, threw his blanket over his shoulders, and set off to climb the peak.

When he reached the top, he stood on the rim of the world. He could see forever and his heart swelled with pride. Then he heard a rustle at his feet, and looking down, he saw a snake. Before he could move, the snake spoke.

"I am about to die," said the snake. "It is too cold for me up here and I am freezing. There is no food and I am starving. Put me under your shirt and take me down to the valley."

"No," said the youth. "I am forewarned. I know your kind. You are a rattlesnake. If I pick you up, you will bite and your bite will kill me."

"Not so," said the snake. "I will treat you differently. If you do this for me, you will be special. I will not harm you."

The youth resisted awhile, but this was a very persuasive snake with beautiful markings. At last the youth tucked it under his shirt and carried it down to the valley. There he laid it gently on the grass, when suddenly the snake coiled, rattled and leapt, biting him on the leg.

"But you promised . . ." cried the youth.

"You knew what I was when you picked me up," said the snake as it slithered away.

---- ■ ----

Wait to read the moral until after the group discussion (step 2).

Moral

And now, wherever I go, I tell that story. I tell it especially to the young people of this nation who might be tempted by alcohol and other drugs. I want them to remember the words of the snake: **You knew what I was when you picked me up.**

---- ■ ----

BUILDING ASSETS, REDUCING RISKS
Duplicating this page is illegal. Do not duplicate without publisher's written permission.

159

Substance Use Disorder Definitions

Substance Use Disorder

Following are some signs and symptoms that may indicate a person has a substance use disorder. The person

- uses alcohol or other drugs in larger amounts or for longer periods of time than intended

- tries to stop or cut down, but is not able to on his or her own

- spends a great deal of time trying to obtain and use the substance as well as recover from the effects of the substance

- has a craving or strong desire or urge to use the substance

- has experienced problems at home, at work, or at school related to his or her substance use

- continues to use the substance despite experiencing social or personal problems caused by this use

- uses substances even in situations where it is physically dangerous

- uses substances despite knowing that he or she is experiencing physical or emotional problems because of the use

- experiences tolerance—needing an increasing amount of the substance to feel the same effect

- experiences withdrawal symptoms when trying to stop using

Someone with two to three of these symptoms may have a mild substance use disorder.	Someone with four to five of these symptoms may have a moderate substance use disorder.	Someone with six or more of these symptoms may have a severe substance use disorder.

1 of 2

BUILDING ASSETS, REDUCING RISKS

Those who have a mild substance use disorder may be able to stop using without help. Even if someone is at the mild level, he or she should stop using, before the use gets worse.

People at the moderate to severe level may be "addicted" to the substance and not able to stop on their own. They may need outside help to quit. Addiction is a lifelong disease, but it can be managed by getting help and stopping the use.

Denial

One of the chief characteristics of a substance use disorder is denial. Denial is the refusal to admit substances are harming the user's health, relationships, and performance in school or work. Denial often is heard in statements like "I don't have a problem," "I can handle it," or "I can quit anytime I want."

Blackout

A blackout is a period of time (seconds, minutes, hours, or days) during which the person using alcohol or other drugs is awake and active but later remembers nothing about it.

Overdose

Overdose is the use of alcohol or other drugs in an amount that is capable of causing psychosis, convulsions, coma, and even death. Due to increased tolerance, substance users have a greater risk for overdosing.

Alcohol Poisoning

Alcohol is a depressant, meaning if it is taken in large amounts, it can slow breathing and heart rate. If too much alcohol is consumed at one time, alcohol poisoning can occur, where the person's respiration and heart rate slow down to the point of death.

Treatment

A process where a person with a substance use disorder gets help to stop using alcohol and other drugs, and learns how to live a healthy and fulfilling life without substances. Some people go to inpatient treatment, where they stay at the treatment center for a period of time. Some people go to outpatient treatment, where the person lives at home but attends treatment sessions during the day. Treatment programs are available at hospitals, clinics, and treatment centers.

2 of 2

Recognizing a Substance Use Disorder

Below are some examples of how a substance use disorder can progress over time. Each level has its own characteristics but tends to lead to the next level.

LEVEL ZERO: This person does not use substances at all.

LEVEL ONE: This person most likely does not have a substance use disorder.

- Does not plan to use alcohol or other drugs; use usually happens when someone offers the substances
- Uses occasionally on weekends with friends or at parties
- Does not experience substantial behavior or attitude changes

LEVEL TWO: This person most likely has a mild substance use disorder.

- Uses substances more regularly, on school nights as well as on weekends
- Begins to buy his or her own alcohol or other drugs
- Begins to use other substances in addition to alcohol and marijuana
- Begins to lose interest in hobbies and school activities, especially sports; grades begin to drop
- Begins lying to parents to hide his or her use of alcohol and other drugs

LEVEL THREE: This person most likely has a moderate substance use disorder.

- Tries to get drunk or high most of the day every day—in the morning, on the way to school, and after school; is preoccupied with getting drunk or high
- Drops non-using friends and avoids family members
- Frequently gets into trouble at school (truancy or fights)
- May resort to stealing to support increased substance use
- Begins using substances alone rather than with friends

LEVEL FOUR: This person most likely has a severe substance use disorder

- Uses alcohol or other drugs to avoid the pain that now comes from not using; there is a loss of control over use
- Needs larger amounts of substances to feel the desired effect
- Worries about running out of a supply of alcohol or other drugs
- Finds it almost impossible to stay in school or hold a job
- Begins to experience poor health condition—loses weight, looks sick, is tired all the time
- May experience blackouts and is at a high risk for death by overdose or suicide

1 of 3

Recognizing a Substance Use Disorder
Exercise

Divide into groups of four to six participants. Your group will be inventing and then describing a stereotypical teenager. The fictitious teenager will belong to one of the five levels of teenage substance use; your class facilitator will assign a level of use to your group. Do not reveal to other groups which level you have been assigned.

In your small group, work together to complete the description of your teen by answering the questions below. When your group has finished developing your fictitious teenager, elect a spokesperson who will read your description to the larger group.

The large group will try to guess which level of substance use is being portrayed. Be creative—do not use information from your handouts word for word. Make the description interesting and challenging for other class members to identify.

Teenager's name: _____

Sex: _____ (M) _____ (F)

What does this teen look like (clothes or hair)?

_____

How would this teen's friends describe him or her?

_____

_____

_____

How does this teen get along with his or her family?

_____

_____

_____

What does this teen do after school?

_____

_____

_____

How do this teen's teachers describe him or her?

_____

_____

_____

Are there any recent changes in this teen's life?

_____

_____

_____

How is his or her general health?

_____

_____

_____

Any other information?

_____

_____

_____

BUILDING ASSETS, REDUCING RISKS

Session 33: Enabling

- 30 minutes

- Boundaries and Expectations
- Social Competencies

- Increase in social skills

- Understanding Enabling handout
- Pens or pencils, one per participant

- Print and copy the Understanding Enabling handout, one per participant.

Purpose

To understand enabling; enabling is defined as anything a person does that causes someone's alcohol or other drug use to continue or get worse

Instructions

1. Conduct a large group discussion using the following questions:

   - What is enabling? Why might someone be an enabler?

   - What are some ways that people enable others?

2. Distribute the Understanding Enabling handout and a pen or pencil to each participant. Review the information on page 1 of the handout with the class.

3. Divide the large group into pairs. Ask participants to work with their partner to complete the exercise on page 2 of the handout.

4. Reconvene the large group and ask the pairs to share their responses to the exercise. Anticipate that there will be differences of opinion and a variety of perspectives on how to respond to the situations on the handout. Encourage participants to consider the various perspectives. Use the following answer key as needed during the discussion.

BUILDING ASSETS, REDUCING RISKS

Duplicating this page is illegal. Do not duplicate without publisher's written permission.

165

Understanding Enabling Answer Key

1.	Your friend missed soccer practice because he was getting high. You told the coach he wasn't feeling well.	3 or 5
2.	You see drugs in your friend's car, but you don't say anything.	3, 4, or 5
3.	You encourage your friend to get high for the first time.	1
4.	You let your friend copy off your test because she has been drinking on week nights.	3, 4, or 5
5.	You know your friend is drinking too much, but you know he can stop when he wants, so you are not worried.	2
6.	Your friend asks you for some money because she owes it to her drug dealer. You give her the money.	3, 4, or 5
7.	Your friend tells you it's impossible to become addicted to cocaine, so you try it for the first time.	2
8.	You offer to get beer for some friends.	1, 3, or 5
9.	You know your friend has a serious drug problem, but you don't encourage him to see a counselor.	3, 4, or 5
10.	Your friend tells you she thinks she drinks too much. You tell her not to worry because everyone parties a lot in high school.	1

Optional Follow-Up

Throughout the school year, remind participants of what enabling is and the problems associated with it.

Grades 6–8 Adaptations

- Instead of asking the class what enabling is, explain what enabling is, and then continue with the question "Why might someone be an enabler?"

- On the Understanding Enabling handout, have the participants work together as a large group on the exercise instead of in pairs.

BUILDING ASSETS, REDUCING RISKS

Understanding Enabling

What Is Enabling?

Enabling is anything a person does that causes someone's alcohol or other drug use to continue or even get worse. Most often, enabling is done by shielding the user from experiencing the consequences of his or her behavior.

The School of Hard Knocks

Hard knocks are unpleasant consequences. We often consider consequences, especially unpleasant ones, as being bad. The truth is that unpleasant consequences are important. They teach us that we have made a poor decision, and they keep us from making the same choice in the future.

The Ways That People Enable

We enable others to continue using alcohol and other drugs when we cover for them, make excuses for them, lie for them, and even take over their responsibilities. These are things we do that enable use. However, we can also enable by what we don't do. Failing to openly and caringly express our concern to a friend we know who has an alcohol or other drug problem is another way of enabling.

Reasons Teenagers Enable

1. Misery loves company: Come on and try it; then we can hang out together more.

2. Inaccurate information: Don't worry, only adults can be alcoholics.

3. Concern about the user's anger: I know everyone is going to be high at the party, but if I don't go he'll be really mad at me.

4. Not knowing what to say or do: I'm concerned about my friend's alcohol use, but I don't know what to say that will be helpful.

5. Concern that you will lose the person's friendship: If I tell my friend what I really think, I might lose her as a friend.

1 of 2

Exercise

With your partner, work on the following exercise together.

The following are examples of teenage enabling. Next to each statement, show which of the reasons for enabling is likely at play by writing 1, 2, 3, 4, or 5 corresponding to the five reasons listed on page 1. There can be more than one reason for each situation.

_____ 1. Your friend missed soccer practice because he was getting high. You told the coach he wasn't feeling well.

_____ 2. You see drugs in your friend's car, but you don't say anything.

_____ 3. You encourage your friend to get high for the first time.

_____ 4. You let your friend copy off your test because she has been drinking on week nights.

_____ 5. You know your friend is drinking too much, but you know he can stop when he wants, so you are not worried.

_____ 6. Your friend asks you for some money because she owes it to her drug dealer. You give her the money.

_____ 7. Your friend tells you it's impossible to become addicted to cocaine, so you try it for the first time.

_____ 8. You offer to get beer for some friends.

_____ 9. You know your friend has a serious drug problem, but you don't encourage him to see a counselor.

_____ 10. Your friend tells you she thinks she drinks too much. You tell her not to worry because everyone parties a lot in high school.

Session 34: Circles of Support

TIME NEEDED

• 30 minutes

ASSET CATEGORIES

• Positive Values

• Support

• Boundaries and
Expectations

RISK/PROTECTIVE FACTORS

• Opportunities for
pro-social involvement

MATERIALS NEEDED

• Post-it Notes,
two per participant

• Pens or pencils, one per
participant

PREPARATION NEEDED

• Set out Post-it Notes
and pens or pencils.

Purpose

To identify and recognize the importance of circles of support

Instructions

1. Ask for a volunteer to stand in front of the class. This person will be identified as a leader to class participants.

2. Ask the other participants to write qualities of leadership on Post-it Notes (such as dependable and responsible).

3. Ask the participants to place the Post-it Notes on the leader in an appropriate location.

4. When all Post-it Notes have been placed on the leader, remove the notes one by one and read the "posted" qualities of leadership aloud to the large group.

5. Divide the large group into four smaller groups—one group representing friends, one family, one community, and one risky behaviors. The person who was the "leader" should not be included in a group.

6. Ask the whole group to brainstorm some risky behaviors.

7. Ask each group to form a tight circle around the identified leader. The circle closest to the leader should be the group representing friends, the second circle should form around the first circle and represent family, the third circle should form around the second circle and represent community, and the final, outer circle should represent risky behaviors.

8. Once everyone is in place, the risky behaviors group should try to break through the circles of support. The circles of support (friends, family, and community) should try to resist and protect the leader. Remind participants there is no roughhousing and this is not a competition. Rather, this activity is a visual demonstration of the importance of circles of support.

BUILDING ASSETS, REDUCING RISKS

Duplicating this page is illegal. Do not duplicate without publisher's written permission.

169

NOTES

9. Lead a large group discussion using the following questions:

- What did this exercise represent? What did it symbolize?

- How did you feel as a friend?

- As a family or community member?

- How did you (ask the leader) feel as the risky behaviors tried to get you?

- What is important about each group? Why is it important to have each of these circles of support?

- How do risky behaviors get through?

- Is there a "lesson learned" or a moral to this exercise?

▶ **Facilitator note: Weave the following statements into the exercise or use as a summary.**

- Although leaders have remarkable qualities, anyone can still be vulnerable to risks.

- Even with the best of intentions, sometimes risky behaviors still get through.

Optional Follow-Up

Throughout the year, remind participants of their circles of support.

Grades 6–8 Adaptations

- Post a master list of commonly known leadership qualities and then encourage participants to brainstorm a few others.

- Name the risky behaviors to make the idea less abstract. Perhaps the circle of risky behaviors is people who want to get you to cheat, for example.

Section 10: Dreams

Session Title	Session Description	Materials Needed	Preparation Needed
Session 35: Dreams	Through an activity and writing exercise, participants strengthen a positive self-identity.	• Paper, one sheet per participant • Pens or pencils, one per participant • Soft music	• Be prepared to play soft music. • Set out paper and pens or pencils.
Session 36: Closure	Through this activity, participants bring a sense of closure to the year.	• Ball of string	• None needed.
Session 37: Celebration	Through this game, participants celebrate the end of the semester, reminding them of the I-Time activities that occurred during the year.	• Dreams Celebration document • Scissors • Paper, several sheets for every five to six participants • Pens or pencils, one for every five to six participants • Whiteboard or Smart Board • Marker • Clock • Bowl or hat	• Write out the Rules for Pictionary on a whiteboard or Smart Board. • Print the Dreams Celebration document.

BUILDING ASSETS, REDUCING RISKS

Duplicating this page is illegal. Do not duplicate without publisher's written permission.

171

Session 35: Dreams

TIME NEEDED

• 30 minutes

ASSET CATEGORIES

• Positive Identity

RISK/PROTECTIVE FACTORS

• Develop positive
  future plans

MATERIALS NEEDED

• Paper, one sheet
  per participant

• Pens or pencils,
  one per participant

• Soft music

PREPARATION NEEDED

• Be prepared to play
  the soft music.

• Set out paper and
  pens or pencils.

Purpose

To strengthen participants' positive self-identity

Instructions

Part One

1. Ask participants to form two groups. Each group should form a circle and stand shoulder to shoulder.

2. Ask all participants to turn to the right so they are facing the back of the person in front of them. They should be close enough that participants can lean backward without falling.

3. Ask every other person to place their hands on the shoulders of the person in front of them.

4. On the count of three, ask the participants who have hands on their shoulders to gradually lean backward. Their partners should try to gently hold them up with their hands.

5. Instruct everyone to stand back up and turn to the left. Repeat the exercise, so the people who were supporting others are now leaning. Then thank everyone for holding each other up.

6. Remind the participants of the support they have in their classmates.

Part Two

1. Ask all participants to pick up a sheet of paper and a pen or pencil before returning to their desks.

2. Play soft music while asking participants to recall the personal goal-setting activity completed earlier in the year (session 9).

3. Explain that today's activity is to create a dream list. Each participant will create a dream list that could include

   • everything he or she would like to become

   • every place he or she would like to go

   • things that he or she would like to achieve in her or his lifetime

   This dream list should not recognize any barriers (money or location). It should truly be dreams. Allow at least ten minutes for this activity.

4. Ask participants to pick one of their dreams and, on the back side of the paper, to list the steps needed to achieve that dream.

5. Ask participants to share their dreams and the steps needed to achieve them with a partner. Have the partner suggest additional steps or ideas that might help the person reach that dream.

Optional Follow-Up

Identify historical figures who have achieved their dreams. Encourage participants to also identify personal goals and dreams throughout the year.

Grades 6–8 Adaptations

No adaptations are needed.

Session 36: Closure

TIME NEEDED

• 30 minutes

ASSET CATEGORIES

• Support

RISK/PROTECTIVE FACTORS

• Bonding and
attachment to school

MATERIALS NEEDED

• Ball of string

PREPARATION NEEDED

• No preparation is needed.

Purpose

To bring a sense of closure to the year

Instructions

1. Ask the large group to form a circle.

2. Have one person hold the ball of string and share one
positive experience about being in this I-Time group
this year (an I-Time activity, a facilitator, a friend). The
person then passes (throws) the ball of string to another
participant in the circle while continuing to hold the
end of the string. The procedure continues until all
participants have shared one positive experience and a
web is created.

3. Read the following words of Chief Seattle:

All things are bound together.

All things connect.

What happens to the Earth
Happens to the children of the Earth.

Man has not woven the thread of life.

He is but one thread.

Whatever he does to the web,
He does to himself.

— Chief Seattle, 1856

4. While participants are holding the string, lead a large group discussion using the following questions:

- What is meant by the words "All things are bound together. All things connect"?

- How does this relate to school? To family? To friends?

Optional Follow-Up

Throughout the year, remind participants of their connections to friends, family, and community.

Grades 6–8 Adaptations

No adaptations are needed.

NOTES

Section 10: Dreams

Session 37: Celebration

Purpose

To celebrate the end of the semester, reminding participants of the I-Time activities that occurred during the year

Instructions

1. Divide participants into teams of five or six members. Give each team several sheets of blank paper and a pen or pencil.

2. Read the Rules for Pictionary with the class:

——————— Rules for Pictionary ———————

- The person drawing can't speak.
- No signs or symbols can be used, although you can use numbers.
- If the team guesses part of the concept, the representative can write that part.
- "Sounds like" can be used.
- Each team is allowed one minute to draw.
- After the correct answer is identified, the entire team stands and states it to the large group.
- The person drawing is rotated.
- The winning team gets one point.

3. Ask each team to send a representative to the facilitator at the front of the room.

4. Each team's representative draws a Pictionary slip from the hat (each group will have a different I-Time activity).

TIME NEEDED

- 30 minutes

ASSET CATEGORIES

- Support

RISK/PROTECTIVE FACTORS

- Opportunities for pro-social involvement

MATERIALS NEEDED

- Dreams Celebration document 37-1
- Scissors
- Paper
- Pens or pencils, one for every group of five or six participants
- Whiteboard or Smart Board
- Marker
- Hat or bowl

PREPARATION NEEDED

- Print the Dreams Celebration document and cut apart the slips. Fold the slips in half and place them in a hat or bowl.
- Write out the Rules for Pictionary on a whiteboard or Smart Board.

5. The representatives return to their groups.

6. At the signal from the facilitator, the representatives have one minute to draw their topic on a sheet of paper or a whiteboard. The first team to correctly guess the topic that their representative is drawing stands and says the answer. This team scores one point. The facilitator tracks the points for each team and is also the timekeeper.

7. Repeat the activity, rotating the representative from each team to ensure all team members have a turn to draw.

8. Play for as long as time allows or until you run out of topics.

Optional Follow-Up

Throughout the year, remind participants of I-Time activities and what they learned.

Grades 6–8 Adaptations

No adaptations are needed.

Dreams Celebration

House Rules	"Do You Know Your Neighbor?"
Commonalities	Shields
Getting Acquainted	Building a Neighborhood
Crossing the River	Person of the Year
Personal Goal Setting	Decision-Making
Leadership Style	Nonverbals
Straw Towers and Create a Game	Feelings Charades
Communication	Trust Dodgeball
Effective Communication	Responding Skills
Learning to Listen	What Is on Your Plate?
Refusal Skills	Support Web
What Are Your Assets?	Grief and Loss
Golden Nuggets	Values
Bullying	Dreams
Fishbowls	Taking the Human Rights Temperature of Your School
Risky Behavior	Risky Behavior Skit
Substance Use	Enabling
Circles of Support	Celebration
Closure	

I-Time Energizers

These three- to five-minute energizers can be used to begin I-Time sessions, they can fill extra I-Time sessions, or they can be used to inject energy into I-Time sessions.

Positive Climate

Back-to-Back

1. Ask two participants to sit on the floor back-to-back, interlock their arms, and place their knees up with their feet flat on the floor. At the signal, ask them to "use each other" to get up without putting their hands on the floor.

2. Try a group of four locking together, then a group of six, and finally groups of eight locking together. Have the end people interlock one arm to form a circle.

3. Discuss the importance of "working together" with everyone using each other's backs for support and working as a unit.

Three Changes

1. Have participants pair up and stand facing each other about two to three feet apart. When a signal is given, they have ten seconds to observe the other person's physical appearance, such as clothing or jewelry.

2. Have them turn back-to-back and discreetly make three changes in their appearance. (For example, participants could move their watch to their other wrist or untie their shoes.)

3. When ready, participants turn and face each other again and see if they can identify the three changes.

4. Discuss how physical changes are fairly easily seen. Mental and emotional changes are not so apparent. We need to be aware of changes in others so we can offer support and help when needed.

BUILDING ASSETS, REDUCING RISKS
Duplicating this page is illegal. Do not duplicate without publisher's written permission.

179

Group in Motion

1. Call a participant to the front of the class.

2. Tell her to make one movement and one sound (e.g., arm moving and saying "click, click").

3. This participant repeats the movement and sound.

4. A second participant comes up and connects his body in some way to the first and makes his own movement and sound and continues to repeat.

5. One at a time, each participant comes up, connects herself or himself to the machine (the line of participants), and continues to make her or his movement and sound. Videotape this process and show it back to the participants!

Koosh Ball Group Juggle

1. Ask all participants to form a circle.

2. Explain that the Koosh ball (or other soft ball) will be passed from one person to another. The main objective of the game is for participants to remember who gave them the ball and to whom they gave it.

3. Ask all participants to raise their hands.

4. Pass one Koosh ball to a participant in the circle.

5. Instruct the first participant to pass the ball to a second participant and then to lower her or his hand.

6. The last participant to receive the Koosh ball should throw it to the facilitator.

7. Make sure everyone knows who his or her two people are—clarify if need be. Then tell the group to get ready to start the group juggle.

8. Now pass nine or ten Koosh balls to the first person in quick succession.

9. Participants should pass the balls on when they receive them. Remind them to receive the ball from the same person and throw to the same person every time.

Highs and Lows

1. Start the session off with five or ten participants or the entire group sharing a high (one good thing they are proud of) and a low (one thing they're really not happy about or that has been bringing them down).

Koosh Ball Story

1. Pass a Koosh ball around the room and whoever receives it adds three words to a fictional, creative, and/or humorous story. Start it, for example, by saying, "This old toad . . . !" Participants who have something to add to this crazy story can raise their hand to receive the Koosh ball. Start new sentences anytime. You'll get some doozies!

Animals

1. Ask participants to select an animal that describes them the best and then explain why (for example, I am most like a bear because I like to sleep when it's cold outside).

Star Search

1. Ask participants to find an object (either outside or in the room) that symbolizes them. They then share what they identified and why.

Rare Birds

1. Distribute the Rare Birds handout to each participant.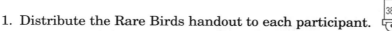
2. Ask all participants to choose at least one category listed on the handout and write how they are unique in that category. (Participants may choose to complete more than one category.)
3. Instruct participants to complete their answers, fold the paper in half, and return it to the facilitator.
4. Throughout the year, choose a Rare Birds sheet, read it to the class without revealing which participant completed the form, and ask the group to guess the author of the handout.

BUILDING ASSETS, REDUCING RISKS

Duplicating this page is illegal. Do not duplicate without publisher's written permission.

181

Communication

Telephone Wire

1. Ask participants to form a circle.

2. Have one person whisper a sentence or two to the person next to him or her. The message can only be said *once*.

3. The person who heard the message then passes it on to the next person.

4. This repeats until the last person receives the message.

5. The last person in the circle says out loud what he or she heard to see how close it comes to the original message.

Feelings

Ball Toss

1. Ask participants to toss around a soft ball and tell how they feel and why. Expressing feelings is always a safe way to begin a group, class, or training.

Support Climate

Name Whip

1. Ask participants to form a circle (perhaps with their desks).

2. Have one participant start off by stating his name and one adjective that describes him that has the same first letter as his name. For example, "Hi, I'm Talented Tom."

3. The second person introduces Tom, and then states her own adjective and name.

4. The third person introduces the first two participants and his own adjective and name. This continues around the circle until the last person tries to remember everyone's adjective and name in the group.

Values

Mentors

1. Ask participants to talk about the person in their lives who has influenced them the most and why.

2. Ask group members to talk about positive learning experiences they have gained from their mentors.

Fun Way to Form Groups

Whistling

3. Determine how many participants are in your class and divide that number by six. This is the number of times you will write the song titles below on pieces of paper.

4. Cut the paper into slips, fold them in half, and place them in a bowl.

5. Have each participant draw a slip of paper and begin whistling or humming the tune of the song written on the paper.

6. Participants will then join with others who are whistling or humming the same tune. Those participants with the same tune form a group.

Song Titles:

- "Jingle Bells"
- "Mary Had a Little Lamb"
- "Row, Row, Row Your Boat"
- "Old MacDonald Had a Farm"
- "Three Blind Mice"
- "Happy Birthday"

BUILDING ASSETS, REDUCING RISKS

Duplicating this page is illegal. Do not duplicate without publisher's written permission.

183

Rare Birds

Name _____

From the following categories, select one in which you feel you are unique. **Write down specifically what makes you unique in that category. Put your name on the paper, fold the paper, and turn it in to the facilitator (without allowing anyone to see what you wrote).**

Throughout the year, the facilitator will draw a paper from this collection, **read it to the group, and ask them to guess who this Rare Bird might be. You may choose more than one category.**

Surprising facts:

_____

Interesting job:

_____

Favorite food:

_____

Interesting experience:

_____

Special awards:

_____

Special skills:

_____

Special interests:

_____

BUILDING ASSETS, REDUCING RISKS

List of Documents on the CD-ROM

Read Me First

Handout 3-1:   Commonalities

Handout 7-1:   Master Grid for Crossing the River

Handout 8-1:   Person of the Year

Handout 9-1:   Personal Goals

Handout 9-2:   Goal Tree Example

Handout 9-3:   Your Personal Goal Tree

Handout 10-1: ABCDE Decision-Making Model

Handout 10-2: Decision-Making

Handout 11-1: Leadership Packet

Handout 13-1: Nonverbal Cues

Handout 15-1: How Do You Feel Today?

Handout 15-2: Feelings Charade

Handout 16-1: Techniques Used to Improve Communication

Handout 16-2: I-Messages

Handout 16-3: Practicing I-Messages

Handout 18-1: Qualities of a Good Listener

Handout 18-2: Please, Just Listen

Handout 19-1: Responding Skills

Handout 19-2: Practice Situations for Reflective Listening

Handout 20-1: Refusal Skills

Handout 22-1: Asset Checklist

BUILDING ASSETS, REDUCING RISKS

Duplicating this page is illegal. Do not duplicate without publisher's written permission.

185

List of Documents on the CD-ROM *continued*

About the Author

Angela Jerabek, MS, is a licensed K–12 teacher and middle school and high school counselor at St. Louis Park High School in Minneapolis, Minnesota. She is a nationally known speaker and educational innovator. Along with *Building Assets, Reducing Risks,* she has developed numerous educational programs and directed evaluation projects in schools across the United States. Her expertise and passion lie in high school reform, youth development, school safety, counseling adolescents and families, and data-driven decision making in schools.

Building Assets, Reducing Risks was created in 1998 to combat the problems of failing grades, substance use, truancy, and discipline referrals taking place at a Minneapolis-area high school. Within one year of implementation, the course failure rate at that school decreased from 44 percent to 28 percent and has remained at 14 percent for the last fifteen years. Since 1998, Ms. Jerabek has been refining the model based on current educational research and recording similar outcomes in suburban, rural, and urban schools. *Building Assets, Reducing Risks* has undergone stringent evaluations including a randomized controlled trial, and the results have been shown to be highly statistically significant.

BUILDING ASSETS, REDUCING RISKS

Duplicating this page is illegal. Do not duplicate without publisher's written permission.

187

As part of the Hazelden Betty Ford Foundation, Hazelden Publishing offers both cutting-edge educational resources and inspirational books. Our print and digital works help guide individuals in treatment and recovery, and their loved ones. Professionals who work to prevent and treat addiction also turn to Hazelden Publishing for evidence-based curricula, digital content solutions, and videos for use in schools, treatment programs, correctional programs, and electronic health records systems. We also offer training for implementation of our curricula.

Through published and digital works, Hazelden Publishing extends the reach of healing and hope to individuals, families, and communities affected by addiction and related issues.

For information about Hazelden publications,
please call **800-328-9000** or visit us online at **hazelden.org/bookstore**.